TRIALS OF THE MOON

REOPENING THE CASE
FOR HISTORICAL WITCHCRAFT

Daniel Hopfer (1470-1536) *Drei Hexen verprügeln den am Boden liegenden Dämon.*
Etching 22.3 × 15.6cm. Private collection.

TRIALS OF THE MOON
REOPENING THE CASE FOR HISTORICAL WITCHCRAFT

BEN WHITMORE

A CRITIQUE OF RONALD HUTTON'S
THE TRIUMPH OF THE MOON
A HISTORY OF MODERN PAGAN WITCHCRAFT

Whitmore, Benjamin John, 1977–
Trials of the Moon: Reopening the Case for Historical Witchcraft. A critique of Ronald Hutton's Triumph of the Moon: A History of Modern Pagan Witchcraft. —1st ed.
Includes bibliographical references and index.

ISBN 978-0-473-17458-3

Published by Briar Books
Auckland, Aotearoa New Zealand

"Take me in that black troop, how long is it since I was there? . . . my dear dove, it is an age since I drank from that good old wine of Tokaj, that we drank in the black troop, give me a glass of that."

—From the trial of Győrgy Gémes, 1739, Hódmezővásárhely, Hungary.
(Pócs 1999 90)

Contents

Stars and black holes

Ronald Hutton is the first academic historian to have attempted a full-scale history of modern Pagan witchcraft (particularly Wicca), and his scholarly yet entertaining tone in *The Triumph of the Moon* has star-struck a generation of Pagans[1] and substantially changed the way we see ourselves. For some, *Triumph* has become a cornerstone of faith, perhaps read alongside Hutton's other books on paganism. It has greatly encouraged intellectual forms of Paganism and witchcraft in which the Gods are regarded as 'thoughtforms' created by people, rather than the other way around. And if Hutton is correct that our Gods and our mode of worship have no precedent in any prior religion, there hardly seems to be any other conclusion. His thesis is that modern Pagan witchcraft is entirely a new invention, cobbled together by a few eccentrics of the early twentieth century out of themes from Romanticism and the recent European occult revival, all supplemented with plenty of imagination, and with no link or even resemblance to any prior form of witchcraft or pagan spirituality. He also contends that since paganism was rapidly eradicated in the Middle Ages,[2] Early Modern witchcraft could not have been a form of paganism — in fact, he claims, witchcraft never existed at all, outside of fantasy, until Gerald Gardner established the religion of Wicca in the early 1950s.

While I agree that today's witchcraft is largely a reinvention, I disagree with several of Hutton's supporting claims, and believe his case is overstated and deeply

---

[1] I adopt Hutton's convention of distinguising contemporary Paganism (capitalised) from earlier historical paganism.

[2] He first argued this in *The Pagan Religions of the Ancient British Isles*, stating that most of southern and western Europe was thoroughly Christianised by the sixth or seventh centuries, and that although paganism was reintroduced to Britain during the Viking invasions, it was finally extinguished there and in the Scandinavian kingdoms during the eleventh century. Lithuania was the last bastion of paganism to fall, in the fourteenth century (1991 258, 261–4, 247, 280–3, 300). In *Witches, Druids and King Arthur* he adds that traces of paganism may have lingered among the Saami of Scandinavia until the seventeenth century (2003a 137). Hutton emphasises that not only was conversion rapid, it was *complete*: "it may be concluded that the official conversion of the British Isles to Christianity left no surviving pre-Christian religions, either in remote areas or as 'underground' movements." (1991 324)

misleading. I had little inkling of this when I first read *Triumph* in 2001; indeed I very much enjoyed the book, though I was uneasy about a few of the conclusions, and noticed a number of errors and oversights. I might have largely accepted his findings, had I not just read another scholarly work on the history of the European witch-trials: Carlo Ginzburg's *Ecstasies: Deciphering the Witches' Sabbath*, which arrives at radically different conclusions regarding the nature of historical witchcraft and its relation to older pagan spirituality. Whom should I believe? At the time I could find no literature critiquing *Triumph* — indeed, it seemed no-one had anything but praise for it — so I resolved to do a little research and write a brief review myself. Nine years later that brief review has grown into this book.

As I began to track down Hutton's sources and compare with other works in the field, I realised that my initial impression of him was wrong: rather than just following common academic consensus, he is a maverick historian with a provocative new take on the history of witchcraft and paganism. And his take is far more conservative than most. In part, this may be explained by his natural affinity to the English school of witchcraft history, which (in the words of Diane Purkiss) had "hardened into an orthodoxy" since the 1970s and largely ignored recent developments by Continental and American historians.[3] I believe we see an example of how such insularism manifests in Hutton's treatment of Ginzburg's work. Though he refers to Ginzburg repeatedly, his apparent unfamiliarity with Ginzburg's ideas and his choice of criticisms against him suggest strongly that he has cribbed from fellow-countryman Norman Cohn's critique and not read Ginzburg himself (or not in any detail). Yet even Cohn's scepticism regarding the reality of Early Modern witchcraft is surpassed by that of Hutton.

Hutton does bring some strong skills to his work. His ability as a story-teller is vast, and he has woven from the unruly tangle of occult history a single narrative that is not only intelligible but entertaining. For someone writing a work of this scope, and pioneering a new academic field in the process, this is quite an achievement. And despite the challenge he presents to the traditional Pagan view of history, he shows considerable sensitivity to our spiritualities — which has earned him a warm welcome in the Wiccan and Pagan communities. I've heard numerous accounts of how thoroughly nice a man he is, and how generous to other researchers. I believe Hutton is genuinely sympathetic to modern witches and Pagans, and that his acute scepticism is — paradoxically — intended to establish our faiths with a greater credibility: he sees Wiccan and Pagan 'creation myths' as obstacles to our being taken seriously, and feels that if we abandon our historical claims we can make a stronger case for the validity of our faiths purely in terms of their spiritual, ethical and social value. Unfortunately, while this may suit true *Neo*pagans who feel no strong ties to the past,

---

[3]Purkiss 1996 59–60.

it disenfranchises many others who feel kinship and connection with that which has gone before. I recall one rather sad conversation I had with a bright young High Priest and High Priestess who were abandoning the Craft because *Triumph* had convinced them they were living a lie.

Clearly, Wicca as we know it is a recent creation,[+] and its 'traditional' history as stated by Gardner is a myth — as has long been recognised by Wiccans — yet I am not convinced that it has no connection or resemblance to historical witchcraft or folk magic. I hope to show that Hutton's word on the subject is far from final, for despite its five-star reviews *Triumph* is riddled with big black holes. Large sections of the book — entire chapters, even — are one-sided, misleading, or plain wrong.[5] Many of his sources are misrepresented, and for a surprising number of his claims he provides no evidence at all, such as his alarming assertion that there was never an Earth Mother goddess in Mesopotamia, Anatolia or Greece.[6] His character-portraits of earlier scholars make for very entertaining reading, and can often give the impression that they and their theories (and even entire fields of research) are untrustworthy and devoid of merit — but his actual evidence against them is often slight. One must always be careful when evaluating a source or theory (academic or otherwise), but Hutton has become mascot to a belief now taken up by many Pagans, that to even consider certain authors and ideas is to openly invite ridicule.

This is all a tremendous pity, because some sections of *Triumph* really are a triumph. Chapters 12, 15, 16 and 17, dealing with the years after Wicca emerged to public view, stand out for their balanced and comprehensive reporting. This is also the period best documented by Wiccans and Pagans themselves, and Hutton has compiled a large number of such sources and extended them with considerable field work of his own.[7] He has also made a real contribution to the study of popular literature, by compiling a broad selection of modern literary depictions of paganism and witchcraft. Indeed, the opening chapter is wonderful, a vivid portrayal of the deep reverence

---

[+]In a sense, it is more recent even than Gardner's time: Wicca continues to grow and evolve as a living tradition, so that the liturgy and ritual inherited from Gardner are now a small but central component.

[5]— despite Hutton's claim that the book contains "no conscious subterfuges, circumlocutions, half-truths, or significant silences" (Hutton 1999a x).

[6]Hutton 1999a 36. Many Pagans have swallowed this whole, putting them in the rather odd position of being more sceptical of the existence of such goddess-cults than most historians in the field — despite being goddess-worshippers.

[7]Hutton still makes some surprising statements regarding this era: his analysis of British Wicca as a right-wing ideology that desired "a free market, in magic and sex as in economics" (p. 361) left me scratching my head, and his statement that Vivianne Crowley became informal successor to Alex Sanders in leading the Alexandrian tradition (p. 373) is palpably wrong: if anyone can be said to hold this position it is Maxine Sanders. Crowley *was* initiated into Maxine's coven, and is thus part of the Alexandrian family, but she only stayed for a short time before seeking re-initiation into Gardnerian Wicca, which has seemingly been her focus ever since. To say that she and Leonora James were "moon and sun of the British Wiccan world" in the 1990s seems equally dubious, though I agree their work was inspirational.

for Classical deities and nature expressed by popular authors from the eighteenth to early twentieth centuries.[8] His reliance on popular literature (in any era) is actually one of the most striking features of the first half of the book, and makes it a valuable and engaging reference for when various pagan and occult ideas filtered into the mainstream, and what became of them there. But while he occasionally traces these ideas back further, more often he barely acknowledges — or altogether denies — that they may have had a prior existence of a less overt nature — which makes his account fundamentally flawed as a history of things occult, esoteric, subcultural or countercultural.

These disagreements aside, Hutton's ultimate aim is laudable: he is trying to clear aside the old myths of Wicca and Neopaganism and establish a solid foundation on which future research can be built.[9] Yet he has exceeded that goal, for he has also swept aside significant unresolved questions, significant contrary evidence and whole fields of potential inquiry. To make untidy areas of the past just disappear is not 'cleaning up history'; it is creating a new myth to replace an old one. I feel it is high time that Wicca and Paganism be permitted to have not just myths, but a history as well.

---

[8] I suspect this reverence was a direct continuation of the pagan revival that was so central to the Italian Renaissance (which we shall discuss later; see also Godwin 2005 and Pennick & Jones 1995 200–3).

[9] A number of Wiccan and Pagan scholars precede Hutton in this endeavour, and have already made good inroads. The publicly visible work of authors such as Doreen Valiente, Margot Adler, Nigel Pennick, Julia Phillips, Don Frew and Mario Pazzaglini (and more recently, Philip Heselton, Michael Howard and Fred Lamond) is just the tip of the iceberg. There has been much unpublished research within the Wiccan community.

Not a single pagan was persecuted during the witch-trials

Part of the pleasure of reading *Triumph* is in marvelling at Hutton's encyclopedic knowledge of history, covering both the mainstream and the deeply esoteric, and the full period from distant prehistory to the current day. This seemingly superhuman feat was, I found, marred by some rather odd errors, which made me dig deeper; and as the errors multiplied I began to wonder how familiar he really was with his material. Most of his statements have supporting citations, but I have discovered several instances in which his sources are not represented faithfully: either vital evidence from these works is ignored which could have altered the conclusions, or in several cases authors are attributed with views they never express.

The most striking example of this happens to coincide with one of Hutton's most pivotal arguments: he claims that by the time of the witch-trials there was no paganism still surviving in Europe to be construed as witchcraft, and thus accused 'witches' could not have been pagans. His support for this is to cite a series of authors who he feels champion this view. Now, to deny the existence of a large-scale organised pagan resistance movement such as postulated by Margaret Murray would make sense. But to deny *any element* of pagan religious practice is a much bolder claim. Checking these authors myself, I found that what they actually say is often quite different.

The first author cited is the early-twentieth-century scholar C. L'Estrange Ewen, whose "close and comprehensive use of. . . archival material. . . left no room for doubt that those tried were not pagans".[10] This is a surprising statement, for Ewen's thesis was no more plausible than Murray's. He too claimed that witchcraft represented a "rival religion" to Christianity with hundreds of thousands of adherents; that religion, he claimed, was Satanism.[11] Even if we leave aside his visions of mass evil-doing, perverted Christian rites and alliance with the Anti-Christ, Ewen uses his sources

---

[10] Hutton 1999a 198.

[11] Ewen 1933 21–3.

to depict a continuity of witchcraft and sorcery from earlier pagan practices: idol-worship, sacrifice to 'demons' or 'devils', well-worshiping and other "vain practices" carried on at sacred trees or stones — and he makes no suggestion that such "hea-thenism" was ever eradicated.[12] On the contrary, he states that although Satanism grew out of Christianity, it was then adopted by "heathen cults desiring more im-pressive supplications than old wives' charms".[13] And despite all this, Ewen agrees with Murray that witchcraft could manifest as "a joyous religion" in certain times and places.[14]

Hutton next rallies together the combined clout of seven prominent witchcraft historians of the 1970s — E. William Monter, Bengt Ankarloo, H. C. Erik Midelfort, Alan Macfarlane, Gerhard Schormann, Bente G. Alver and Robert Muchembled — who he says have "left no doubt that the people tried for witchcraft in Early Modern Europe were not practitioners of a surviving pagan religion".[15] Let's examine what each of them actually say:

E. William Monter, for a start, maintains that many "witches" held beliefs firmly rooted in pre-Christian paganism. He suggests that the 'coloured devils' of the French woods were originally pagan deities, for instance, and that the obscure local saints to whose shrines white witches sent invalids on curative pilgrimages "were often local pagan deities with a Christian veneer."[16] Is this not a description of vestigial pagan religion?

The second of this group of authors, Bengt Ankarloo (I have not read his book in Swedish, but rather, later essays in English), distances himself from "the dogma of learned origins" — the theory that witchcraft testimonies were shaped by learned theologians and interrogators through cultural infiltration of their ideas and leading questioning, and that it is useless to look for popular origins. Rather, he accepts the theory of Ginzburg, Gustav Henningsen and Gábor Klaniczay that a "pre-Christian, shamanistic substratum" existed in many parts of Europe and contributed to beliefs surrounding the witches' sabbath.[17]

---

[12] Ewen 1929 1–9.

[13] Ewen 1933 24.

[14] Ewen 1933 25.

[15] Hutton 1999a 362. The works cited are: Macfarlane (1970) *Witchcraft in Tudor and Stuart Eng-land*; Ankarloo (1971) *Trolldomsprocesserna I Sverige*; Alver (1971) *Heksetro og Trolldom*; Midelfort (1972) *Witch-hunting in South-Western Germany*; Monter (1976) *Witchcraft in France and Switzerland*; Muchembled (1977) *Sorcieres du Cambresis*; Schormann (1977) *Hexenprozesse in Nordwestdeutschland*; and Dupont-Bouchet, Frijhoff & Muchembled (1978) *Prophetes et Sorcieres dans le Pays-Bas*.

Elsewhere throughout *Triumph* Hutton mentions a number of theories connecting residual pagan-ism with witchcraft — mostly quite dated — and either dismisses them *as though* they were invalid (but without explaining *why*), or else criticises their methodology while not providing evidence for his own opposing position. This may lead the casual reader to think he has made a strong case.

[16] Monter 1976 p. 112; p. 175, quoting from Delcambre's *Devins-guérisseurs*, 139ff.

[17] Ankarloo & Henningsen 1989 5–6, 7, 13; Ankarloo 1989 305.

American historian H. C. Erik Midelfort charts at some length how witchcraft beliefs developed out of pre-Christian paganism (for instance, the theme of riding out at night on the backs of animals in the company of Diana, described as a "pagan error" in the ninth-century canon *Episcopi Eorumque*, turning into riding in the company of the devil by the fourteenth century[18]), as well as from anti-pagan ideas of diabolical power and satanic pact that started forming from Christianity's first arrival in Europe. He highlights the "superstitious magical beliefs and practices [that] were common among both village and city folk", but doubts whether these ever culminated in organised group ritual.[19]

Alan Macfarlane, though not actively contradicting Hutton's assertion, doesn't support it either. In his introduction he dismisses Murray's organised underground pagan cult as "too sophisticated and articulate for the society with which we are concerned [Essex]", though he agrees with her that accusations should be treated as "something more than intolerant superstitions". Beyond this, his interest is in the mechanics of societal persecution, not the actual beliefs of the accused, whose philosophical and religious outlook he makes no attempt to discover. As he explains it, "This study is mainly concerned with showing how witchcraft functioned, once the basic assumptions about the nature of evil, the types of causation, and origins of supernatural 'power' were present."[20]

Gerhard Schormann, on the other hand, affirms that surviving ancient forms of worship could at times be prosecuted under charges of witchcraft.[21] Likewise, he cites a number of German trials in which folk magic was denounced as witchcraft.[22] In general, though, Schormann regards 'witchcraft' as an imaginary offense, with its most characteristic elements — the pact, the Sabbath, sexual intercourse with demons and so on — being inventions of the late Middle Ages.

Bente Alver and Robert Muchembled were difficult for me to check directly, as my understanding of Norwegian and French is rudimentary, and the books cited by Hutton are not available in translation. I have only found a few passages of Bente Alver in English translation, but these appear to contradict Hutton's position that accused witches "were not practitioners of a surviving pagan religion". Read, for ex-

---

[18] Midelfort 1972 15–19.

[19] He is not certain of this, though: "At Carcassonne and Toulouse, confessions referred to secret meetings of sorcerers who worshipped the devil in animal form and practised various kinds of harmful magic. Whether such groups or secret organizations ever existed in any form is exceedingly difficult to determine." (Midelfort 1972 1, 18)

[20] Macfarlane 1970 10–11. See also Ginzburg's summary of Macfarlane (1990 3–4).

[21] Schormann cites Carlo Ginzburg's study of the northern Italian *benandanti* as a convincing example: "Das Fortleben antiker Kultformen und ihre schließliche Verfolgung mittels Hexenprozessen ist ja grundsätzlich nicht auszuschließen: Ginzburg hat einen solchen Vorgang in einem bestimmten Gebiet überzeugend dargestellt - darüber gleich Näheres." (Schormann 1996 102–3)

[22] Schormann 1996 107.

ample, her account of the witch-trial of a Sami magician, as summarised in a collection of Scandinavian folklore:

> The Lapp Quive Baardsen was clearly a specialist in making sailing wind by magic. His services were sought by the community. From the trial transcript, it appears that when his practice resulted in the death of some of his clients, however, he was legally held responsible. Quive Baardsen describes how the Lapps used their rune drums to put themselves into trances in which to communicate with the spirit world. In the eyes of the court, these practices must have seemed heretical; they were reason enough to condemn the accused to death.[23]

With Muchembled I have relied on a later essay in English,[24] and he, for once, seems partially in agreement with Hutton, holding that the elements of popular culture and social reality that fed into witchcraft stereotypes "have nothing to do with any organized non-Christian cult, even of a residual or mythic kind." (Note, though: he only discounts *organised* forms of cult.) As Ankarloo and his colleague Gustav Henningsen summarise him, Muchembled is

> in line with the position of the seventies, when he regards the sabbath as 'simply and solely a figment created by theologians, whose ideas governed the imagination of the élite classes of Europe in the late Middle Ages'. But he parts with the dogma of learned origins when he states that the demonologists' description of the sabbath 'was a diabolized version of practices, customs and beliefs which really existed among peasant folk . . . with the difference that every one of its features is given a negative coefficient'[25]

So, while not affording these folk practices the status of an organised cult or religion, Muchembled at least affirms their existence and the antipathy of theologians towards them. As examples of such practices, customs and beliefs, he describes the night-time revelries of inhabitants of Artois and Flanders, which involved fights between armed youths and wild dancing in isolated spots in the wee small hours. He also describes popular superstitions and spells such as the lists of 'mighty names' that soldiers carried for protection.[26]

---

[23] A summary of Bente Gullveig Alver (1971) *Heksetro og trolddom* 116–19, given in Kvideland & Sehmsdorf 1988 193. Alver's 2008 book *Mellem mennesker og magter* (in Danish) explores popular Norwegian beliefs in magic and elves, beliefs that were essential in ordinary people's lives in the sixteenth and seventeenth centuries. She explores the ambiguity between good and evil magic, and the rôles both personal guilt and accusation played in causing popular magic to be interpreted as witchcraft.

[24] Muchembled 1989.

[25] Ankarloo & Henningsen 1989 5–6.

[26] Muchembled 1989 149–152.

The major achievement of these seven authors of the 1970s was not in establishing that accused witches were not pagans; rather, it was in demonstrating how a number of societal factors converged in the Early Modern Age in different parts of Europe to precipitate moral panic and full-blown hunts.[27] That a conflict between Christian and pre-Christian belief systems may have been one of these factors is in no way precluded; on the contrary, it is specifically stated by several of these authors, as we have seen.

In a more recent polemic with Pagan researcher Jani Farrell-Roberts, Hutton repeated his assertion that these seven authors had "left no doubt that the accused were not practitioners of a surviving pagan religion", and he recommended for his Pagan audience three short paperbacks that would disabuse them of such falsehoods and acquaint them with recent developments in the field.[28] It may be instructive to digress here and quote from one of these paperbacks, by P. G. Maxwell-Stuart, at length:

> Europe at this time [in the 14th and 15th centuries], one must
> remember, was not the monolithic Roman Christian entity of myth

---

[27] I shall briefly summarise the common contributing factors for interested readers, taking them from Maxwell-Stuart (2001): Although witch-trials peaked during roughly the same period throughout most of Europe (c.1580–c.1660), the precise reasons for these persecutions differed from area to area (p. 55). Fundamentally, each local witch-craze represented a breakdown in the previous tolerance for popular forms of magic, inspired by a new doctrine that even beneficent forms of sorcery were accomplished through complicity with Satan. (At that time there were few people who didn't seek the services of a magical operator at some point in their lives, or use magic charms themselves.) As such, the concepts of diabolical pact and Satanic conspiracy were grafted onto popular sorcery (pp. 14–15, 26–7, 71, 75–6). Fear of witches was increased by the widespread belief that the end of times and the final battle against Satan was approaching, and Protestant and Catholic rivalries only served to strengthen this (pp. 16–17, 43–44). The use of folk-magic to protect against magical attack was itself forbidden, and under Protestantism the Church no longer provided counter-charms either, so those who believed themselves victims of witchcraft were forced to seek legal action instead (pp. 52–3). The transition in most areas from 'accusatorial' to 'inquisitorial' legal models meant fewer obstacles to accusation; simultaneously, because eye-witnesses to diabolism were so difficult to find, witchcraft became a *crimen exceptum* for which torture (avoided for most other crimes) was commonly licensed to obtain a confession: this was the only means, absent witnesses, of determining guilt. This led to a much greater likelihood of conviction, as well as implication and subsequent trial and torture of others (pp. 23–5, 57), so much so that we hear of two villages in Germany where only two residents were left alive at the end of a spate of trials (p. 56). In some areas confiscations of property awarded to 'discoverers' of witches gave a financial incentive; elsewhere economic difficulties brought by wars (and by extended crop failures in Germany) increased the general mood of desperation. This was all fed by tracts of fanatical propaganda, often emphasising women's tendency to irrationality and wanton lust and thus their particular susceptibility to ensnarement by Satan (pp. 60–63).

[28] Hutton 2003b. The books are: G. Scarre & J. Callow (2001) *Witchcraft and Magic in Sixteenth and Seventeenth Century Europe*; P. G. Maxwell-Stuart (2001) *Witchcraft in Europe and the New World 1400–1800*; and J. Sharpe (2001) *Witchcraft in Early Modern England*.

and popular assumption. Large tracts of it had scarcely been converted more than skin-deep, whole areas were still to all intents and purposes pagan, and since the purpose of the missionaries was to win over pagans from both their native religions and their magical practices, there was a tendency to run paganism and magic together and treat them as though they were more or less the same. Nevertheless, official views and interpretations of popular beliefs and practices remained relatively fluid for a while, as can be seen from learned debate over witches' ability to fly. But during the fourteenth century in particular official attitudes were beginning to harden, and it would not be long before Church and state would decide that in magic they were faced by an adversary not so much eccentric as hostile. The principal reason is straightforward. The concept of a demonic pact was being grafted on to popular magical practices and this changed them fundamentally from being private acts done for personal advantage or malicious gratification to potential assaults upon the foundations of Church and state.[29]

Maxwell-Stuart expands on this theme of pre-Christian beliefs and magic throughout the book, pointing out that a large proportion of accused witches were actually magical healers or diviners (such as English cunning folk);[30] that Scottish 'witches' were in many cases people who claimed to have met and had dealings with fairies (reinterpreted as evil spirits);[31] that paganism persisted throughout much of Scandinavia alongside first Catholicism then Protestantism, and became a particular target of witch-trials from the 1600s on;[32] that Russian witch-trials were largely an attempt to eradicate popular magical practices in a region never more than partially Christianised;[33] and that until the 1700s Transylvanian 'witches' mostly came under suspicion for performing traditional fertility rites or healing magic.[34] I can only endorse Hutton's recommendation: the book is indeed a fine introduction to current scholarly consensus in the field of witchcraft history, and a very easy read, at only 110 pages.

Returning to *Triumph*, Hutton's final blow is to describe "a tidal wave of accumulating research which [in the 1990s] swept away . . . any possibility of doubt regarding the lack of correlation between paganism and early modern witchcraft".[35] How-

[29] Maxwell-Stuart 2001 23.

[30] Maxwell-Stuart 2001 26, 68–72.

[31] Maxwell-Stuart 2001 27.

[32] Maxwell-Stuart 2001 78–80.

[33] Maxwell-Stuart 2001 83–4.

[34] Maxwell-Stuart 2001 85.

[35] Hutton 1999a 377.

ever, his "tidal wave" includes authors such as Wolfgang Behringer, Carlo Ginzburg, Bengt Ankarloo, Gustav Henningsen and Robin Briggs, who have effectively argued that there *was* some correlation between witchcraft and pagan beliefs, at least in vestigial form.[36] For Hutton, though, the case is closed: "not a single person tried for witchcraft in Europe between 1400 and 1800 has been demonstrated to have adhered to a pagan religion."[37]

Exactly what constitutes 'pagan religion' is problematic, and we shall more closely examine Hutton's take on this later on. But his statement as a whole is misleading. The survival of pre-Christian belief systems and their contribution to the diabolised stereotype of witchcraft in the Early Modern era has become widely accepted in the field of witchcraft history. It has been amply demonstrated by a whole school of well-respected historians, including Éva Pócs, Gustav Henningsen, Carlo Ginzburg, Gábor Klaniczay, Wolfgang Behringer and Juhan Kahk (studying witchcraft in Hungary, Sicily, Italy, Eastern Europe, Bavaria and Estonia, respectively), and other luminaries.

What these authors have established is that beliefs about magic followed remarkably consistent, well-developed patterns throughout Europe, and that while they operated within the social framework of Christianity they were anything but Christian in origin. It is true that many accused witches were simply ordinary people caught up in the machinery of societal paranoia, but there were others who truly believed themselves to be mediators between the living and the dead, able to bless, curse and prophesise. Like shamans they would leave their bodies in spirit (often in animal form) to visit the meadows of the dead, feast with the fairies, or fight among the clouds. Many held intense devotion for a goddess figure, a 'good mistress' or a 'Queen of the Fairies'. It was around ecstatic beliefs such as these that the diabolised stereotype of the witches' sabbath coalesced.[38]

---

[36] Briggs states that while Murray grossly misinterpreted the evidence, she "had a point in stressing that there were pagan survivals involved" — "The persecution really did stem from the universal peasant belief in occult personal powers" (Briggs 1995 57–8). Behringer devotes an entire book, *Shaman of Oberstdorf* (1998), to explaining how surviving elements of pre-Christian spirituality, magic and festivity in German peasant culture became distorted into accusations of witchcraft. Regarding Ginzburg, see below. All these authors are, of course, united in denouncing Murray's thesis of a coordinated pagan sect in opposition to Christianity, and perhaps this denunciation is the "tidal wave" that Hutton perceives.

[37] Hutton 1999a 380.

[38] Ginzburg 1990 Part 2, ch. 1 (Ginzburg, who pioneered this school of research, is arguably still its most important author). Compare with Hutton's remark in *Pagan Religions* that "Dr. Murray's ignorance of ancient paganism in Western Europe prevented her from realizing that the rituals imputed to early modern witches were not antique rites but parodies of contemporary Christian ceremonies and social mores." (1991 303)

What is a witch?

Despite such a large body of evidence surrounding ecstatic magical traditions in Europe, they barely get a mention in *Triumph*. This conspicuous absence is not explained, but I believe the reason can be found in Hutton's earlier book, *The Pagan Religions of the Ancient British Isles*. Here he briefly mentions a few of these traditions before stating that they are inadmissible as evidence of a surviving mediæval pagan religion. His basis for this is an anthropological study on Rhodesian witchcraft:

> Among the Shona in the 1950s and 1960s were found women who freely admitted to going abroad at night and to destroying other humans by magic. When cross-examined rigorously by sceptical British authorities, they were proved to have dreamed these things (having become obsessed with them because of the suspicions of their neighbours) and become persuaded that what they imagined in their sleep was occurring in reality.[39]

Thus, we are told, the British and European ecstatic traditions, centring as they do on out-of-body experiences, are also merely fantasies: they are *passive experiences* rather than *actively held* belief systems. However, this argument is unsustained and unconvincing. The European data cannot all be put down to dreams, guilty self-doubt and imagined transgressions, for many of these people saw themselves as benefactors, not malefactors (it was only as diabolical stereotypes progressed that more and more of these people became convinced they were pitted against the rest of society[40]), and

---

[39] Hutton 1991 307–8. This, a summary of Cohn's argument (1975 176–9), is not even a fair appraisal of the Rhodesian evidence, as there were those who actively pursued otherworldly experiences rather than just passively dreaming them. Take, for example, the three Shona women who declared that they met naked near a stand of trees and rubbed their hands and faces with a 'medicine for night witching', a salve prepared from certain powdered roots. "I felt things going very dark, and felt as though I wanted to vomit", one explained; "On each occasion we travelled about naked and we appeared to travel through the air. I remember three kraals we visited..." (Duerr 1985 1, 134)

[40] Ginzburg 1983 28, 31, 123–4, 135; 1990 10; Henningsen 1989 204–7. As Maxwell-Stuart explains it, Church and state officialdom and 'the rest' were drawing apart in their beliefs, "and as they did so 'the

their testimonies speak of great pride and self-certainty as well as *conscious deliberation*. Furthermore, their activities were not limited to the world of dreams. The northern Italian *benandanti* worked magic and made predictions for others in their communities; they consciously prepared for their regular spectral journeys which they made during quarterly festivals (the Ember Weeks) and warned their spouses not to move their vacated bodies while their spirits were travelling. It is unknown whether they ever congregated for physical meetings.[41]

The Romanian *călușari* had remarkably similar beliefs to *benandanti* and *did* physically congregate.[42] They have survived to the present day as a highly ritualised magical society, with complex dance and theatre forms, magic circles cast with a sword, healing and fertility rites, ritual possession, strict secrecy surrounding certain magical procedures, and initiatory oaths of fidelity taken at the edge of a stream or pool in the presence of the female divinity Irodeasa (now 'Saint' Irodeasa), which involve being measured from head to toe with red thread.[43] Another dance tradition this bears an unmistakeable resemblance to is English morris dancing, and there are hints of a shared origin, steeped in the indigenous fairy-lore of Europe.[44] Quite possibly, other European dance traditions such as the Swiss Perchtenlauf, revolving as they do around pre-Christian goddess traditions and fairy-lore,[45] have similar origins. In Calvinist Guernsey and Jersey we find group enactments of 'werewolfery', wild and blasphemous night-time revels containing many features familiar from witch testimonies.[46] We shall discuss these similarities further in a later chapter.

---

rest' became inclined to feel themselves distinct from the Church in particular both in what they were willing to believe and in what they were unwilling to surrender". (2001 23)

[41] Ginzburg proposes that their spectral journeys were dream-like enactments of rituals that were previously enacted physically (Ginzburg 1983 24); we know of at least one instance in which *benandanti* were in communication with each other, physically meeting and planning their activities, later to be performed in spirit (Ginzburg 1983 129–133). We can therefore be certain that these people's spiritual and magical activities were not limited to dreams alone; but even if they had been, should we dismiss them so easily? Dreams are central to the magical and spiritual practices of many cultures — imagine, for instance, telling an Australian aborigine that the 'dreamtime' is not a valid part of their spirituality because they only dream it. Any modern witch or magician, of course, will understand the value placed in the 'astral world', out-of-body experiences and lucid dreaming.

[42] The name *călușari* is only recorded from the twentieth century, but in neighbouring Moldavia we hear of mid-seventeenth-century enchanters and enchantresses called *caluczenii*, who from their name and description clearly represent the same or a very closely-allied tradition. Like the *călușari* they met in groups of seven, nine or eleven and wore feminine clothing; in ecstasy they leapt as though flying, with drawn swords, and were not punished if they killed anyone; and they healed the sick. (Ginzburg 1990 189–190)

[43] Kligman 1977 11–19.

[44] Kligman 1977 60–61.

[45] Motz 1984.

[46] Ogier 1998. In European folklore there is much cross-over between the themes of werewolf and witch, and the two often seem virtually synonymous (see Pócs 1999 129–134 for survey and analysis of werewolf types; see also Ginzburg 1990 154, Motz 1984 159–160).

So do any of these traditions count as 'witchcraft'? While Hutton never actually defines the terms 'witch' or 'witchcraft',[47] he appears to borrow their definitions from the field of anthropology, without explaining to his readers the precise technical meanings they have in this field, or the difficulties of applying those meanings to British and European data. The anthropological 'witch' is someone whose maleficium stems from an in-dwelling and intangible quality of evil, a quality that even they themselves may be unaware of; they express this maleficium through equally intangible means, such as dreams or the 'evil eye'. A 'witch' differs from the anthropological 'sorcerer' in that they do not employ (or else leave no trace of) magical ritual, tools or materials.[48] In other words, the terms 'witch' and 'witchcraft' are used in situations where it could be perceived as all coming down to fantasy. Such 'witches' are typically the creatures of fairytale, nightmare and societal paranoia, and those who confess as witches under these terms may indeed be ordinary people who have fallen victim to suggestion. When anthropologists transplant this English word to foreign cultures they are harking back to the antiquated view that British and European witchcraft was an imaginary crime, or at most, a scam for extorting money and favours.[49] That understanding has since changed. While many accused 'witches' in Europe were doubtless ordinary people unlucky enough to get swept up in the storm, for others we know that magic and otherworldly interactions were fundamental to their beliefs and even their identities.

The inappropriateness of the anthropological definition (as regards England at least) is underlined by Keith Thomas:

> In general . . . the anthropological distinction between witchcraft
> and sorcery is of limited utility when applied to England. It can be said
> that the sorcerer used material objects, whereas the witch did not. But
> the presence or absence of magical techniques does not seem to have
> been of great concern to those who took part in the trials. . . .
> The historian cannot even say, with the anthropologist, that sorcerers
> existed, whereas witches were imaginary. For some of those accused of
> being witches really had tried to harm others by mere ill-wishing, un-
> accompanied by magical techniques. In intention, at least, witchcraft

---

[47] He does however carefully define 'religion', and partially defines 'Paganism' (capitalised) and 'paganism' (1999a xii, 3–4).

[48] Macfarlane 1970 310, summarising Evans-Pritchard (1937 21).

[49] The Shona word *muroyi* is rendered 'witch' in the Rhodesian Witchcraft Suppression Act of 1899, which draws heavily on the English Witchcraft Act of 1735 and treats witchcraft as a fantasy or "pretence" in the same manner. J. R. Crawford followed this usage in his Rhodesian study. Crawford also cites the term's usage in Evans-Pritchard's famous study of witchcraft among the Azande people (Crawford 1967 5, 8, 73; Appendix II), though Evans-Pritchard cautioned that his choice of terms was arbitrary, based more on expediency than on any close correspondence between English and Azande concepts (Evans-Pritchard 1937 8–9).

was not an impossible crime.[50]

Even if we were to accept these European magical traditions as 'witchcraft', it might still be argued that we have not demonstrated the survival of any "pagan religion": was this true paganism, or merely a residue of paganism translated into the realm of popular magic? P. G. Maxwell-Stuart, as quoted earlier, distinguishes between religion and magic, and thus implies that magic can be independent of faith. Hutton has previously expressed the same opinion.[51] And indeed, despite their unorthodox beliefs, our European magical practitioners often maintained that they were operating within the bounds of the Christian faith. We have numerous testimonies of this throughout Europe, such as from the Italian *benandanti* who said they fought "for the faith of Christ", the Livonian 'werewolf' who claimed "we are God's dogs", or the Scottish 'witch' who believed he was in contact with God's angel 'Christson-day'.[52] On the other hand, official Christianity was antagonistic to their beliefs, just as the Catholic Church is to Vodou and Santeria today, even though adherents of those faiths claim to be Catholic. So can we consider them pagan if they considered themselves Christian?

We shall return to this question later, but in reality this whole question of semantics, though interesting, is tangential to Hutton's argument. His aim is simply to deny that 'real' witches or 'real' witchcraft played any part in the Early Modern witch craze or the developing sabbath stereotype: the most he allows is that witchcraft "could, at times, be a self-impowering [sic] fantasy for the dispossessed".[53] To hold such an extreme view one must ignore the obvious: across Europe there were folk-magicians and folk-magic that actually fitted the bill rather well. Whether or not they called themselves 'Christian', whether or not they engaged in organised group rituals, they were the aboriginal folk magicians of Europe, and were known, among other things, as 'witches'.

---

[50] Thomas 1997 464–5. According to Ankarloo and Henningsen, European witchcraft is just as difficult to compare with the African data, and much that has been considered 'peculiar' about England is actually characteristic of large parts of Europe: "Sixteenth-century Europe was not an African village." (Ankarloo & Henningsen 1989 1, 14) Macfarlane's view is similar: "although anthropologists have provided some useful analytic distinctions, these do not really help in a number of societies. . . . words like 'witchcraft' and 'sorcery' were used in a number of different senses in seventeenth century England." He explains that 'witchcraft' could equally refer to harming and healing, malevolent and beneficent magic, and that he himself applies it to malevolent magic only as a convenience. (Macfarlane 1970 Appendix 2)

[51] Hutton 1991 289, 291; this has been contested by Frew 1998. I will discuss the distinction or lack thereof between magic and religion in later chapters.

[52] Ginzburg 1990 97, 153. Accused witches in Sicily were particularly intractable in this belief, one woman even recounting how her mistress the fairy Doña Zabella had brought Catholic priests from Malta to recite a mass at their sabbath (Henningsen 1989 206).

[53] Hutton 1999a 380.

What Great Goddess?

The second chapter of *Triumph* charts the development in literature and scholarship of the theme of a Great Goddess. The whole chapter is built on the assumption that deities fitting this description are entirely modern inventions: Hutton holds that these goddesses (or this Goddess) were dreamt up by nineteenth- and early twentieth-century poets, novelists and historians, and that the historians projected this fantasy onto the historical record, even manipulating data to make it fit. No attempt is made to test this assumption, though Hutton does cite one case of suspected archaeological fraud and one of misinterpretation of data.[54] Such anecdotes perhaps illustrate

---

[54] The former was the Grimes Graves goddess 'discovery' in Norfolk. The latter was Sir Arthur Evans' supposed misattribution of a single goddess figure to both Iraq and Crete, relying on incorrect dating and (we are told) a misreading of the Nippur archæological report (Hutton 1999a 38–9):

> Evans interpreted the report as saying that the deity found in the earliest levels of its first temple was female, and represented by a clay figurine of the sort now familiar to him from Cretan neolithic sites; he concluded that they all represented the same goddess, to whom the Nippur figure was ancestral. Evans had got the chronology the wrong way round (the Cretan data is older), and the book on the Nippur excavations does not in fact decisively attribute the dedication of that temple to a goddess. What in fact happened was that he . . . had projected backwards upon prehistory the goddess who had emerged as pre-eminent in the minds of poets and novelists during the nineteenth century.

In fact, it is Hutton who seems to have misread the report, which mentions no deity or figurine in the chapter he cites, though goddess figurines (unambiguously female) from the mid-third millennium BCE and later appear in other chapters. I am at a loss as to what he is on about. Evans certainly made no claim that the temple was dedicated to a goddess, and while he did suggest a possible derivation between the Nippur and Knossos figurines, he made it clear that this was only tentative and that the dating of the Knossos artefacts was still very uncertain (Evans 1901). When Evans later advanced his theory of a widely-diffused goddess iconography he had the correct dating, as well as the corroboration of a large array of similar figurines from the Aegean, Anatolia, Syria, Mesopotamia, Cyprus and the Balkans — indeed the Nippur data had become a relatively minor detail (Evans 1921 45–52). It seems then that Evans had not "misunderstood" his data, and that his "conversion" was neither hasty nor based on misread second-hand reports; nor indeed is there any evident reason to doubt his findings.

Hutton misrepresents Evans elsewhere, too: he claims that Evans "had failed to find any self-evident interpretation of the nature of the religions" of Malta, and that it was only James Mellaart's "gift for

the popularity of the Great Mother theory but not, as he would imply, its fallacy. We have powerful and plentiful evidence — certain knowledge, in fact — that such goddesses were worshipped throughout large areas and periods of the ancient world. Let's take a closer look at Hutton's arguments, one by one:

According to Hutton, the famed Numidian novelist Lucius Apuleius is unique among the ancients in portraying a goddess (Isis) as the embodiment of all other goddesses, identified with the moon and the whole of nature; all other people believed the various goddesses to be separate personalities.[55] This is completely untrue. By late antiquity Isis was popularly identified with numerous other goddesses[56] and had a huge cult following throughout the Roman Empire and much of the known world. In Pompeii Isis was known as *Panathea* ('All-Goddess'), "in her oneness everything", Isis "of countless names".[57] In Egyptian texts Isis is frequently depicted as the source of all and containing all: The Egyptian Book of the Dead names her "She who gives birth to heaven and earth".[58] Other common epithets attesting to her primordial nature are 'Mother of the Gods',[59] 'Queen of the Gods', 'Great Divine Mother',[60] 'Great Goddess Existing from the Beginning', 'The prototype of all beings'[61] and *'Thiouis'* ('the only one').[62] Plutarch records an inscription from the shrine of Neith-Isis-Athena at Sais: "I am all that hath been, and is, and shall be; and my veil no mortal has hitherto raised".[63] In Greco-Roman tradition she became identified with the moon and the whole of nature. In fact, far from being an innovation, Apuleius' account "replicates themes found in contemporary hymns to Isis having prototypes that date back to the Hellenistic period".[64]

Apuleius himself held initiations and priesthood in several cults and mysteries, among which, it has long been conjectured, were the Mysteries of Isis and Osiris.[65] If so, he affords us a valuable glimpse of Isis as initiates knew her.[66]

---

publicity" that established Çatal Höyük as a Mother Goddess cult centre (Hutton 1999a 280–1). In fact, Evans included Malta in his survey of regions adhering to "the cult, under varying names and attributes, of a series of Great Goddesses who often combined the ideas of motherhood and virginity." (Evans 1921 45, 52).

[55] Hutton 1999a 32.

[56] Among others, she was identified with Artemis, Hecate, Selene, Io, Demeter and Tyche, as well as the Aegean Great Mother, the Phrygian Cybele, the Syrian Atargatis and the Carthagaean Tanit (Witt 1997 72, 149–150).

[57] Witt 1997 72.

[58] Budge 1904 vol. 1, 519; vol. 2, 90.

[59] Witt 1997 131.

[60] Sharpe 1837 91.

[61] Budge 1934 199–200.

[62] Solmsen 1979 51.

[63] Plutarch *On Isis and Osiris* § 9.

[64] Delia 1998 539.

[65] Gollnick 1999 17–19.

[66] Griffiths 1975 6.

Hutton is similarly dismissive of the concepts of either a Great Mother or a Triple Goddess, which he lumps together as a nineteenth century fallacy which swept through academia in a wave of "burgeoning enthusiasm"; but, he tells us, "No temple had been built to her, and no public worship accorded".[67] In that case, the following invocation should come as a surprise:

> Come to me, O beloved mistress, three-faced Selene; . . . You're Justice and the Moira's threads: Klotho and Lachesis and Atropos; three-headed, you're Persephone, Megaira, Allekto, many-formed, . . . they call you Hekate, many-named, Mene, cleaving air just like dart-shooter Artemis, Persephone, shooter of deer, night shining, triple-sounding, triple-headed, triple-voiced Selene; triple-pointed, triple-faced, triple-necked, and Goddess of the Triple Ways, . . . Mother of gods and men, and nature, mother of all things, . . . Beginning and End are you, and you alone rule all. For all things are from you, and in you do all things, O eternal one, come to their end. . . .

This, from a Greek magical papyrus of late antiquity, from Hellenised Egypt, gives us a glimpse into the world of private sorcery.[68] We also know of public, state-supported cults centring on mother goddesses who were simultaneously single and triple; for example, the 'Mothers of Engyon' in Sicily whom Carlo Ginzburg discusses at length,[69] and Hutton (having critiqued his book) should thus be familiar with.

Admittedly, few ancient triple goddesses fit Robert Graves' division into Maiden, Mother and Crone — a scheme widely adopted among Neopagans — rather, the majority of ancient depictions show three women of the same age.[70] But Hutton's scepticism is not directed specifically at Maiden-Mother-Crone triads, or

---

[67] Hutton 1999a 37, 42.

[68] Betz 1992 84–5. Similar invocations can be found in other papyri, also addressed to a supreme goddess of many names. This example is a generic petition to the goddess to aid in any magical endeavour. This kind of magic was quite popular, and the magicians who kept such documents were widely employed by ordinary people throughout the Greco-Roman world to administer "remedies for a thousand petty troubles plaguing mankind: everything from migraine to runny nose to bedbugs to horse races, and, of course, all the troubles of love and money" (Betz 1992 xlvii).

[69] Ginzburg 1990 124–5.

[70] Celtic triple goddesses included the Ériu-Banbha-Fódla trinity, the triple Brigit in Ireland, the Mórrigna, the Machas and the Celtic Matres (Aldhouse-Green 1992 169–70). Fate goddesses associated with childbirth, often in threes and often associated with spinning, are attested across Europe from the Iron Age and also in Bronze Age Anatolia. These include the Greek *Moirae*, Roman *Parcae*, Germanic Norns, Latvian *Láimas*, Russian *Rožanicy*, Czech *Sudičky*, Polish *Rodzanice*, Slovene *Rojenice*, Croat *Rodjenice*, Serbian *Sudjenice*, Bulgarian *Narečnice* or *Urisnice*, Albanian *Fatit, Fatmirat, Mirë* or *Ora*, and Romanian *Ursitoare, Ursitele* or *Ursoiare* (West 2007 379–385; Petreska 2005 225). Around the Mediterranean, duplication or triplication of single divinities was widespread (Ginzburg 1990 124). Some well-known Classical triple divinities include Hecate, the Charites, the Erinnyes and Diana Nemorensis.

even triple goddesses in general, but a whole spectrum of ancient goddess cults proposed from the nineteenth century on, including Great Mothers (Isis and Cybele come to mind), Earth Mothers, triple goddesses and goddesses with dual aspects of virgin and mother.[71] The latter he confidently states is simply the mythographers' own projection of the Virgin Mary onto their source data, although he provides nothing to support this novel (and quite wrong) assertion.[72] One example of an ancient goddess who was both maiden and mother is the Zoroastrian *yazata* Anahita, fertility goddess of waters, who was the ancient Persian 'Great Mother'. She was a virgin, identified by the Greeks with the virgin Artemis, and in fifth-century Armenia her festival was, it seems, re-established as the feast of the Assumption of the Virgin Mary.[73] Artemis herself, though a virgin, was invoked as 'Mother' by women who wished to conceive.[74] The dying and resurrected god Attis was born of Cybele in her form of the virgin Nana, who conceived when a pomegranate was placed on her lap.[75] In some myths the god Dionysus was 'immaculately' conceived: in an Orphic myth Zeus in the form of a serpent begat Dionysus on the virgin Persephone while she was weaving in a cave; in the more well-known myth Semele is the mother, who falls pregnant with Dionysus after drinking a potion made from his heart.[76]

Hutton is at a loss to find an Earth Mother — a goddess identified with both motherhood and the earth — in the Mesopotamian, Anatolian or Greek cultures (the idea that a single Greek Mother Earth was identified with other goddesses and venerated since prehistory he describes as "novel").[77] How about the Anatolian Cybele or the Sumerian Ninhursag?[78] The Greek Earth Mother (whose worship extends from prehistory) appears in such early and mainstream sources as the Homeric

---

[71] Hutton portrays these varieties of goddesses as a succession of imaginative elaborations on the theme, culminating in Robert Graves' triple goddess: "By the time that he [Graves] wrote, the image of his goddess had been developing for about a hundred and fifty years." (Hutton 1999a 42)

[72] Hutton 1999a 36, 37, 40.

[73] Regarding her status as 'Great Mother' see Turner & Coulter 2001 50; for her status as a virgin, see Babayan 2002 134 and the *Ābân Yast* verses 64, 78 and 126 in Darmesteter 1882 69, 72, 82; regarding identification with Artemis, see Verbrugghe & Wickersham 2001 62; regarding the rededication of her feast see Fisher et. al. 1968 804–5.

[74] Mallory & Adams 1997 596.

[75] Leeming 1998 25–6.

[76] Leeming 1998 33, 217.

[77] Hutton 1999a 35–6.

[78] Cybele was Earth goddess and mother of the gods in Phrygia and Asia Minor; from the reign of Augustus she also became extremely popular throughout the Roman Empire as 'Magna Meter' ('Great Mother'), after the oracles predicted that Rome would defeat Hannibal if they took up her worship. Her cult became one of the most important in Rome and she was considered Mother of the state and mother of the state's most important deity, Jupiter (Roller 1999 ch. 10). Ninhursag was the Sumerian "Earth Mother" and "Queen Who Gives Birth". She created mankind from clay, and was wife or sister to Enlil, the principal deity of the Sumerian pantheon (Turner & Coulter 2001 136–7, 168, 346).

hymns:

> Concerning Earth [*Gaia*], the mother of all, shall I sing, firm Earth, eldest of gods, that nourishes all things in the world; . . . Hail, Mother of the Gods, thou wife of starry Ouranos, and freely in return for my ode give me livelihood sufficient.[79]

Gaia is one of the first, primordial gods born of Chaos in Hesiod's *Theogony*, the virgin mother and then wife of Ouranos, mother of Cronus and Rhea, and grandmother of Zeus. Shrines were devoted to her throughout Greece, and her worship was considered the prototype of all piety.[80] Gaia was also prominent in Orphic tradition, where she is "mother of men and of the blessed Gods", and is made synonymous with Hestia, Rhea, Eleusinian Demeter ("goddess of many names"), the Cerealean Mother, Meter Theon ('Mother of the Gods') and (probably) Nature (who is "self-fathered and hence fatherless", "self-sufficient").[81] A typical Orphic verse describes her as "Earth [Gaia], the Mother of all, Demeter, giver of wealth".[82] Orphism, a mystery religion and philosophical tradition renowned for its magic workers and shamanistic rites, is especially interesting to us because it has had such a strong influence on modern mysticism. Neoplatonists such as Marsilio Ficino saw in it the pinnacle of ancient philosophy, and secured it a lasting place in the Western Mystery Tradition.[83]

How could Hutton have missed such prominent and well-attested deities? It turns out he is not oblivious to the existence of Gaia or her Roman equivalent, Terra Mater ('Mother Earth'): in his earlier book *Pagan Religions of the Ancient British Isles*

---

[79] Harrison 1928 62.

[80] Turner & Coulter 2001 184; Hard & Rose 2004 32; Burkert 1985 175.

[81] *Orphic Hymns* numbers 10, 14, 26, 27, 40, 41 (Athanassakis 1988). The Derveni papyrus, dating from c. 340 BCE, explains the merging of these goddesses:

> "Earth (Ge), Mother (Meter), Rhea and Hera is the same (*or*: are one and the same). She/it was called Earth (Ge) by convention; Mother, because all things are born from her (*or*: from this one). Ge and Gaia according to each one's dialect. And (she/it) was called Demeter as the Mother Earth (Ge Meter), one name from the two; for it was the same. And it is said in the *Hymns* too: '*Demeter Rhea Ge Meter Hestia Deio*'. For (she/it) was also called Deio because she/it was torn (*or*: ravaged ἐδηιώθη) in the mixing/sexual intercourse. He will make it clear when, according to the verses, she is born. . . . And (she/it) is called Rhea because many and . . . animals were born . . . from her." (Betegh 2004 47. The ellipses and italics are as given by Betegh; ellipses indicate lacunae in the manuscript.)

See also Betegh p. 222 regarding the antiquity of the *Hymns*.

[82] Diodorus Siculus, Book 1 § 12.

[83] An understanding of Orphic theology, particularly as interpreted by Neoplatonists from Proclus onward, provides important context for the study of modern magical movements. Orphism is also a fine example of the blurring between religion and magic that is so characteristic of esoteric philosophies, but which Hutton claims was inconceivable to any ancient European pagan. (Hutton 1991 335; c.f. Frew 1998)

he asserts that these figures were only ever philosophical abstractions, never deities to be worshipped! This astonishing claim, for which he offers no evidence, is then used to support his argument that mediæval depictions of Terra Mater (as a naked woman suckling animals) do not depict a deity.[84]

The eminent Classical historian Georg Luck expresses his opinion on the Mediterranean cult of the Earth Mother:

> The roots of magic are no doubt prehistoric. There is reason to believe that some fundamental magical beliefs and rituals go back to the cult of the great earth goddess. In historical times, she was worshipped in Greece and other Mediterranean countries under a variety of names: Ge or Gaia, Demeter, Ceres, Terra Mater, Bona Dea, Cybele, Ishtar, Atargatis, and so on. There must have been an important cult of an Earth Mother in prehistoric Greece long before the Indo-European invaders known as the Hellenes arrived. No doubt the ancient Greeks' own Demeter owes something to that pre-Greek deity, and it is conceivable that the parts of the ritual (human sacrifices, for instance) that were rejected later on survived in secret. The fact that iron knives are generally taboo in magical sacrifices suggests that they may have originated in the Bronze or Stone Age. In other cases the Greeks gave a new interpretation to existing sanctuaries of Mother Earth, for instance in Delphi, where they attached to the old Earth oracle, with its prophetess, their god Apollo. The inevitable conflict between an old and a new religion may help to explain why magic, as a profession, remained suspect and feared among the Greeks and why the great witches of Greek mythology, Medea and Circe, are portrayed as evil or dangerous. In fact, they may have been goddesses of a former religion or priestesses of the Mother Earth cult.[85]

The idea of God as female is hardly so novel as to be surprising. To take a leaf from Freud, it seems only natural to me that an all-powerful mother-figure should appeal to at least a few people in any era. So when the "Earth Mother" pops up again in the famous Old English *Æcerbot*, I doubt that this prayer was inspired by Greek mythol-

---

[84] Hutton 1991 316. This mistake (and its lack of referencing) is unfortunately typical of *Pagan Religions*. Greek Gaia's importance as a goddess we have already discussed; her Roman equivalent Tellus or Terra Mater was a major goddess in Roman religion invoked at several festivals throughout the year, and was particularly important to peasant farmers. She had a temple in Rome and received public sacrifice, on one occasion at the hands of Caesar Augustus himself (Berger 1985 19–21; Zancer 1990 169; Crook, Lintott & Rawson 1923 737). Pamela Berger charts the goddess' continued presence through the Middle Ages and her eventual transformation into a number of different saints (Berger 1985).

[85] Luck 1985 5. Luck is a Professor Emeritus at Johns Hopkins University, and his celebrated book *Arcana Mundi* is a standard text in Classics.

ogy.[86] We meet her again in this stunningly beautiful invocation from a twelfth-century Old English herbal:

> Earth, divine goddess, Mother Nature who generatest all things and bringest forth anew the sun which thou hast given to the nations; Guardian of sky and sea and of all gods and powers and through thy power all nature falls silent and then sinks in sleep. And again thou bringest back the light and chasest away night and yet again thou coverest us most securely with thy shades. Thou dost contain chaos infinite, yea and winds and showers and storms; thou sendest them out when thou wilt and causest the seas to roar; thou chasest away the sun and arousest the storm. Again when thou wilt thou sendest forth the joyous day and givest the nourishment of life with thy eternal surety; and when the soul departs to thee we return. Thou indeed art duly called great Mother of the gods; thou conquerest by thy divine name. Thou art the source of the strength of nations and of gods, without thee nothing can be brought to perfection or be born; thou art great queen of the gods. Goddess! I adore thee as divine; I call upon thy name; be pleased to grant that which I ask thee, so shall I give thanks to thee, goddess, with one faith. . . .[87]

Among the ancient Germanic peoples we find Nerthus, the Earth Mother who was anciently venerated as their most important deity and made her annual rounds in a wagon drawn by cows;[88] it is possible that an echo of her survives to this day in the figure of Frau Holda in her wagon, a supernatural being still revered in Germany, Austria and Switzerland under a variety of names, and considered Queen of the witches.[89]

---

[86] This is indeed a proposal of Hutton's, though: "is it [the *Æcerbot*] the work of somebody learned in the Greek texts, from which they had gained Hesiod's myth of the female earth, Gaia, with whom the male sky mated?" (Hutton 1991 294). This is perhaps unlikely, since Greek language, mythology and philosophy were largely unknown in western Europe, even amongst the literati, until the Greek revival at the turn of the fifteenth century (Patrick 2007 684).

The *Æcerbot* ('field remedy') was an elaborate community ritual intended to restore fertility to poorly-producing or blighted land. Hutton sees it as a Christian composition, and it is indeed couched in a Christian framework; however, many elements are regarded amongst scholars as pre-Christian. (Berger 2001 66; West 2007 177) One version of it recorded in a convent at Corvei substitutes "Eostar, Eostar, eorþan modor" for the usual "Erce, Erce, Erce, eorþan modor", introducing the name of a well-known fertility goddess. The usual name Erce is more obscure, but has been tentatively linked to the Germanic Frau Harke, a regional variant of Holda or Perchta (Rohde 1922 39–40).

[87] Rohde 1922 40–41. The translation is by Charles Singer.

[88] Tacitus, *Germania* § 40.

[89] Grimm 1998 vol. I 268; vol. III xx. Also, Rose 2003 111. William P. Reaves' forthcoming book *Odin's Wife: Mother Earth in Germanic Lore* contains new research establishing a more definite connection

Even if we were to set aside current scholarship and evidence, Hutton's claim that all these varieties of 'Great Goddess' were simply figments of the nineteenth-century imagination would stretch the limits of belief, for he requires us to accept that just a century ago, scholars at the head of their field could on the whole be naïve, uncritical dreamers. Perhaps some were, but Hutton would have us dismiss whole eras and branches of scholarship on his say-so. Revisionism of this scale should always provoke caution in a reader.

In countering Hutton's claims I have tried, for the sake of argument, to stick to the particular goddess-varieties he has named: syncretic Great Mothers, triple goddesses, virgin mothers and Earth Mothers. But several of the deities we've discussed fit more than one of these categories, while other closely-related divinities fit none. In fact, the pigeon-holing I have followed in this chapter tends to obscure the similarities between goddesses, which are often far more striking than the differences. If we were to seek these similarities it would soon become apparent firstly how arbitrary such classifications are, and secondly how dense the mythological and cultic connections between ancient goddesses were, and how widespread. Then, I believe, talking about *the* Great Goddess or *the* Earth Mother of antiquity might seem more reasonable.[90] But that discussion must wait for another time.

---

between Nerthus and modern cart- and plough-divinities such as Holda. The excerpts I have read are very compelling.

[90] Or we could follow Pamela Berger, and talk not of a single goddess, but of "diverse realisations of a single magico-religious idea" (2001 1).

Pan and Jesus

In the third chapter of *Triumph*, Hutton turns to the figure of the Horned God. He proposes that this god was born out of popular literary interest in the figure of Pan, but a Pan very different to the relatively minor god of the ancient world ("a Citroen 2CV amongst gods", as he quotes Ken Dowden). Rather, he tells us, this was a Pan raised to pre-eminence among the gods, who died and returned with the seasons, more like a Jesus of the natural world: indeed Hutton believes that the modern Pan and the Wiccan Horned God owe a far greater debt to Christianity than to any pre-Christian religion. This is an explicit rejection of the old thesis of James Frazer, advanced in *The Golden Bough*, that dying and resurrected gods were widespread in the ancient world.

At first glance Hutton's hypothesis, while provocative, is still plausible; however, the evidence he provides for it doesn't stack up. Hutton tells us there is only one example in the Classical world of a dying and resurrected god having developed into a widespread pagan mystery religion: the god Attis, under the Roman Empire, with a relatively tiny number of adherents — and Hutton says this may even have been inspired by Christianity.[91] This is quite untrue. Some of the most famous of the ancient mystery religions centred around such a figure. The Orphic and Dionysian mysteries were based around the repeated death and rebirth of Dionysus (a horned god), who was also widely identified with Iacchus the torch-bearer, a prominent figure in the most famous Mysteries of the ancient world, those at Eleusis.[92] Osiris, revered in

---

[91] Hutton 1999a 43, 122.

[92] This is not to say that Dionysus' death and rebirth featured in the Eleusinian mysteries, although that too is quite possible: 'Brimos', the 'strong child' figuratively born at the height of the *epopteia* at Eleusis, may well have been this same Iacchus/Dionysus, born of Persephone (Parker 2005 357–9). The identification of Iacchus as Dionysus is found (for example) in a Paean to Dionysus inscribed at Delphi, in Sophocles' *Antigone* (Harrison 1991 541–2), in Orphic Hymn 42 (Athanassakis 1988), Strabo's *Geography* 10.3.10, and Nonnos' *Dionysiaca* (1.28ff, 48.848ff). According to Stephen of Byzantium, "the Lesser Mysteries performed at Agra of Agrae were an imitation of what happened about Dionysus" (Harrison 1991 559).

A number of other public festivals celebrated Dionysus' regular seasonal death and his subsequent re-

the widespread Isiac and Osirian mysteries, is killed, dismembered, reassembled, and eventually resurrected as a 'living god', *Osiris Khenti Amenti*, after his child Horus has spilled the last of his enemies' blood.[93] New research by Bojana Mojsov documents how Osiris' resurrection was publicly celebrated in passion plays for thousands of years (his being the most popular and enduring cult of the ancient world), and how direct an influence this cult had on the Christianity that followed. It provided a model not only for Christ's death, resurrection and ascent to heaven as judge of the dead, but also for the Holy Trinity, baptism and the Eucharistic sacrament, along with other customs and mythical details. Osiris was a seasonal fertility god linked with the regular inundation of the Nile, and thus conforms well to Frazer's model. Mojsov also observes that the Osiris myth has been preserved in esoteric streams of philosophy such as alchemy, Rosicrucianism and Freemasonry, thus surviving in esoteric societies to the present day with much of its meaning intact.[94]

Also within the last ten years, major new research has been published by Tryggve Mettinger on the subject of dying and resurrected gods throughout the Mediterranean world in general, which shows that Dumuzi/Tammuz, Baal, Melquert and the west Semitic Adonis all fall in this category. Again, some of these deities carried the same seasonal/agricultural and ritual connotations as in Frazer's model.[95] Indeed, resurrected deities often paralleled the resurrection of crops and of the human soul, and were commonly associated with dominant earth-goddesses, according to Morford & Lenardon's standard textbook on Classical mythology: another corroboration of major elements of Frazer's thesis.[96] Perhaps Frazer wasn't so far off the mark after all?

Although Pan doesn't fit into the usual list of dying and resurrected gods, he is closely associated — at times even identified — with some of the deities we have just mentioned. And we should think twice before passing him off as a minor god.

In the Orphic mysteries of the Hellenistic era Pan is raised to the level of "All-god", synonymous with Phanes-Zeus, the *protogonos* ('first-born'), origin and source

turn from the underworld (Otto 1995 189–201); his grave was said to be in Delphi, where he was buried beneath the *omphalos* (Harrison 1991 557).

[93] Budge 2003 vol. 1 193; vol. 2 10–11; Budge 1934 276. In the Theban recension of *The Book of Going Forth By Day*, Osiris (represented by the deceased) is addressed as follows: "You are a Great One whose strength is mighty, and your son Horus is your protector; he will remove all evil which is on you. Your flesh is knit together for you, your members are recreated for you, your bones are reassembled for you, . . . Rise up, Osiris; I have given you my hand and have caused you to stand up living forever." (Faulkner et. al. 2008 p. 133 §181) The birth goddess Heqet, who takes the form of a frog, assisted Osiris in rising from the dead; the frog was subsequently adopted by Egyptian Christians as the symbol of Christ's resurrection (Budge 1934 97–8).

[94] Mojsov 2005. Thanks to Wade MacMorrighan for alerting me to this author.

[95] Mettinger 2001. Such precedents don't prove the antiquity of the Wiccan Horned God, but they do detract from Hutton's claim that he could only be modelled on the figure of Christ.

[96] Morford & Lenardon 2006 p. 325.

of all things, who formed the world.[97] In the Orphic world-view the *protogonos* is the first of a series of three incarnations of Dionysus (the 'Thrice Born'), their most important god.[98] This Dionysus of Orphic tradition was far more than a god of wine; he was a dying and rising fertility god, the earthly agent of his heavenly father. He was a god of personal redemption who brought salvation to his devotees: freedom from the mortality which is a consequence of humanity's involvement in a primal sin.[99] And he lent various other imagery and mythology to the Christ who followed.[100] So to revise Hutton, why not call Jesus a domesticated Dionysus? But Hutton should know all this, not just from a familiarity with Classics, but also because an entire chapter of *Witchcraft Today* is devoted to discussing these traditions.[101] Perhaps he only read selectively from the founding book of the modern witchcraft revival — or else thought Gerald Gardner's scholarship so poor as not to be worth checking.

Although Pan had relatively little religious importance in most cities of Greece, he was a major god — perhaps *the* major god — in many rural areas. In Arcadia Pan (the "most ancient and most honoured") had a similar prestige to Zeus, and was probably considered his foster-brother. After his decisive intervention in the Battle of Marathon, Pan attracted a strong cult in the city of Athens as well.[102] Major gods in foreign countries were also equated by the Greeks with Pan, as in the case of the Egyptian Khnum, deity of the city of Mendes, who was also known by the Greeks as

[97] In the *Hieronyman Theogony* this figure is Protogonos, Phanes, Zeus and Pan; in the *Orphic Rhapsodies* he is additionally called Metis, Eros, Erikepaios and Bromios (a common epithet of Dionysus). (West 1983 205)

[98] Bonnefoy & Doniger 1992a 165; Parker 1995 490–5. Dionysus was first incarnated as the *Protogonos*, from whom the universe and the first gods emerge; Zeus, on the advice of Night, swallowed the *Protogonos* and assumed his powers, after which he begat the second incarnation of Dionysus (Zagreus) upon his daughter Persephone. Dionysus Zagreus is pursued by the Titans, sent by jealous Hera, and after changing into a succession of different animal forms is torn apart and devoured, but his heart is saved and implanted in Semele: he is finally reincarnated as Dionysus proper, born among men of a mortal mother and a divine father.

[99] Parker 1995 496–8. That sin was complicity in his murder, for the human race arose from the ashes of the Titans admixed with Dionysus' own partially devoured body: hence humans' dual nature of material and spiritual.

[100] For example, the miracle that Jesus performed at Cana, turning water into wine, is commemorated on January 6, which coincides with Dionysus' festival, January 5–6. During this festival springs in Dionysus' temples at Andros and Teos produced wine instead of water; a similar festival of Dionysus at Elis (of unknown date) saw empty pots miraculously filled with wine (Pausanias 6.26.1–2; Athenaeus Book I §61; Pliny the Elder 2.106, 31.13). Dionysus also turned spring-water into wine to intoxicate the beast Agdistis (Leeming 1998 25). As previously noted, Dionysus was immaculately conceived in two versions of his birth-story (Leeming 1998 33, 217). See also Morford & Lenardon 2006 363–4 regarding syncretism of Dionysus and Jesus.

[101] Gardner 2004 ch. 7: *The Witches and the Mysteries*.

[102] Borgeaud 1988 4, 42–43, 176; ch. 7. The Athenian view of the god had a sentimentality remarkably similar to that seen in modern depictions of him (which Hutton believes was born out of Romantic-era poetry): Pan ruled an alluring countryside, as seen from the romanticising eyes of city-dwellers.

both goat-god and All-god.[103]

Hutton does observe that occasional mediæval Christian writers had made Pan a "universal deity of the natural world"[104] (which begs the question: why would a Christian writer promote a *pagan* deity to this status?), however he seems unaware that hermeticists from the fifteenth century onwards also raised the god to this level, including Marsilio Ficino (1496), Francesco Giorgi (1525), Giulio Camillo Delminio (1550), Guy Lefèvre de la Boderie (1578), Clovis Hesteau de Nuysement (in 1621) and Athanasius Kircher (1653). These writers all built on an Orphic model in treating Pan and Jupiter as synonymous, and identifying in this combined figure the unifying force that embraces the manifold, protean shapes of nature.[105]

These hermeticists had a strong influence upon later magical writers, Kircher particularly so: for instance, he popularised the Qabalistic Tree of Life to the non-Jewish world, and his depiction of Pan is repeated almost verbatim in the ritual of the famous Hermetic Order of the Golden Dawn, itself a strong influence on modern Wicca.[106]

So where does Pan fit into European witchcraft? Georg Luck expresses his opinion:

> Finally, when the victorious Christian Church began to hunt witches and wizards, its actions were often directed against surviving pagan cults. In continental Europe, as well as in Britain, some worshippers of the ancient Celtic and Greco-Roman gods had refused to convert to Christianity, and the rites they performed (by necessity in secret) were interpreted as magical rites. The Celts worshipped a horned male god that may have reminded the Romans of the god Pan, a minor god to be sure, but one who could drive you into a "panic" terror when you encountered him at noontime. This combination of horned gods, one Celtic, one classical, produced a very powerful deity around which the *pagani* rallied. Indeed, so powerful was this god that the Christian priests cast him as the prototype of the Devil, with horns, hoofs, claws, a tail, and a generally shaggy appearance.[107]

---

[103] Harrison 1991 651.

[104] Hutton 1999a 44.

[105] Ficino 2008 193; Bonnefoy & Doniger 1992b 215–6; Robinson 2005 335; Godwin 1979 59. The idea that Zeus and Pan were both titles of the all-creating power is attested to in the fifth century CE by Macrobius, quoting a more ancient Orphic fragment (*Saturnalia* I.23.22). A similar hermetic view is expressed by his friend, the pagan Servius (Varner 2006 100–101).

[106] Regardie 1989 213 (vol. II 183–4 in the original edition).

[107] Luck 1985 6–7. Celtic scholar Anne Ross considers the horned god cult in Britain to have been second only in importance to the 'cult of the head' (Ross 1967 ch. 3). Cernunnos was also a favourite deity amongst the Celts of northern Italy, Spain and Gaul, where he was represented in public masked revels

Hutton's stumbling block is that he only does justice to one avenue of research: that of popular, exoteric literature and poetry. By assuming that the origins of Horned God are in popular literature he imposes a selection bias, and ensures that that is all he will find. This over-reliance on popular literature is apparent again when he surveys how often various deities have appeared in popular English poetry, in an attempt to show that the Wiccan Goddess and God didn't predate the nineteenth century. He has substituted a thumb through Eric Smith's *Dictionary of Classical Reference in English Poetry* for a more detailed engagement with historical anthropology and folklore.[108] The fallacy in this approach is easily demonstrated, for if we were to apply the same analysis to the popular poetry of today we would conclude that the ancient gods have been all but entirely abandoned, whereas we know that their worship is stronger now, with the rise of Neopaganism, than it has been for centuries.

---

at the January feast of kalends even into the seventh century, alongside mummery and cross-dressing (MacMullen 1997 37). Late artefacts such as an eighth-century Cernunnos figure at Meigle, Scotland, attest to his continued presence long after the establishment of Christianity; he may even have left literary traces in mythical figures such as Connal Cernach (Ross 1967 143–151). The Celtic stag-god became a prototype for early Christian depictions of Satan as horned, squatting, and bearing a ram-headed serpent (Ross 1967 132, 145).

[108] Hutton 1999a 32, 43. When he itemises the common functions of goddesses of "the pagan ancient world", I suspect this is based on a similar survey. Bizarrely, civic affairs tops his list, followed by justice, war and domestic affairs. Nature and the earth, he tells us, were much less common concerns for goddesses (p. 32; no source or explanation is given). Perhaps he is familiar with some of the more famous Classical texts such as Homer and Virgil (or *Bullfinch's Mythology*): these give a sense of the official, city-state religions at the urban hubs of Classical Greece and Rome, in which major goddesses unsurprisingly had a preponderance with cities, justice, civilisation and learning. But such works are in no way representative of the entire "pagan ancient world". Those Classical authors who recorded rural and foreign customs, such as Pausanias and Herodotus, paint a rather different picture, mentioning numerous local goddesses concerned with the earth, nature and fertility. And even within urban Greece and Rome this picture is typical of little more than the core Olympian pantheon. A host of Titanic, chthonic and primordial divinities, along with hugely popular imported cult goddesses like Cybele and Isis, fall outside Hutton's scheme entirely, being firmly associated with the earth, nature and (in many cases) the irrational.

Cunning folk

Hutton devotes a very colourful and entertaining chapter to the subject of cunning folk — the folk magicians of the English countryside — and although he never says it (and may not intend it), he manages to convey the impression that cunning-craft is a recent phenomenon. In the opening paragraph he does briefly mention a continuity from Early Modern times, but (as I only realised upon careful re-reading) from then on the data he present derive entirely from the late eighteenth century onward. His characterisation of cunning folk emphasises their showmanship and individual eccentricity, while minimising any sense of a coherent tradition. He maintains that they were individual eccentrics who had little or no contact with each other and no detectable consistency in their methods, any similarities being explained by the fact that they purchased their spells from the same mail-order companies; but "Above all, they devised spells according to their own whims and creative talents, and the needs of their customers."[109] English cunning-craft is actually many centuries older than this, and many of the magical techniques employed were widely consistent over large stretches of time and space.[110] Indeed, E. William Monter points out striking similarities with the methods of white witches on the Continent.[111] Cunning folk were certainly very numerous in the period Hutton discusses, but no less so in prior centuries. Around the year 1600 they were thought similar in number throughout England to parish clergy,[112] and Macfarlane's detailed study of Essex shows that not one of its villages was more than ten miles from a known cunning man or woman.

---

[109] Hutton 1999a 92, 97, 98.

[110] Keith Thomas mentions practitioners known by name back to the fifteenth century. He finds some charms to have survived from Anglo-Saxon times, some from Classical or early Christian practice. Although the original meaning of many verbal or textual formulae was unknown to the (mostly illiterate) practitioners, their physical techniques were nonetheless "highly traditional", as were the purposes to which they were applied (1997 181–2, 184).

[111] "In some ways, white witchcraft in Lorraine resembled its British counterpart. Occasionally these similarities extend down to points of detail, as in the method of divination in which a girdle was measured three times, or even in the formulae of some of the curative prayers." (Monter 1976 174.)

[112] Thomas 1997 245.

The forty-one men and women included in his study are, however, "only a fraction of those who actually were cunning folk in Essex": because of the respect afforded to them, few left their mark on the historical record by being brought to court.[113]

Earlier cunning folk were rather different to the intellectual wizards that Hutton focuses on: typically they neither possessed books nor concerned themselves with technical theories of magic such as the hermetic and alchemical philosophies that were circulating amongst the literati; their theories and techniques derived either from mediæval religion or more ancient sources:

> Most of the magical techniques of the village wizard had been inherited from the Middle Ages, and had direct links with Anglo-Saxon and Classical practice.[114]

Despite the fact that some cunning folk were prosecuted as witches,[115] Hutton is adamant that their practices were entirely unrelated to those associated with witches, and he goes to some lengths to always differentiate 'witchcraft' from 'cunning-craft'. Remember, his key thesis is that witchcraft never existed. At one point he even faults Charles Leland for referring to Italian witches as 'witches', and himself translates the old Italian word *stregheria* as "cunning craft".[116] But this attempt to shoehorn Italian sorcery into a term specific to the British Isles is inconsistent with any Italian dictionary, and the distinction he is trying to enforce is not even present in English sources — Alan Macfarlane and Keith Thomas both indicate that the words 'cunning-man' or 'cunning-woman' and 'witch' were largely interchangeable:[117]

> There were a number of interchangeable terms for these practitioners, 'white', 'good', or 'unbinding' witches, blessers, wizards, sorcerers, however 'cunning-man' and 'wise-man' were the most frequent.[118]

The contemporary commentator Reginald Scot notes: "At this day it is indifferent to say in the English tongue, 'she is a witch' or 'she is a wise woman'".[119] Indeed a cunning-person's reputation could lead to accusations of 'black' witchcraft. In England, for instance, some of those accused of being 'white witches' in ecclesiastical

---

[113] Macfarlane 1970 115, 120.

[114] Thomas 1997 228.

[115] Macfarlane 1970 115.

[116] Hutton 1999a 143–4.

[117] Thomas 1997 436–7.

[118] Macfarlane 1970 130. He discusses this further in Appendix 2, and elsewhere gives examples of these usages, such as Robert Burton's statement around 1620, that "Sorcerors are too common, Cunning men, Wisards and white-witches . . . in every village" (p. 115) and Thomas Ady's description of the sorcerers as "Cunning Men, or good Witches" (p. 122).

[119] Scot 1989 V. ix.

courts were later accused of being 'black witches' at the Assizes.[120] Hutton himself includes at least one self-declared 'witch' in his colourful menagerie of eighteenth- and nineteenth-century cunning men and women.[121]

Since *Triumph* was written, British historian Emma Wilby has shown how ambivalent the distinction was between cunning folk and witches in Early Modern Britain, and she argues that many 'witches' convicted of employing 'demon' familiars were in fact cunning folk whose 'fairy' familiars had been demonised by their neighbours or their élite prosecutors.[122] Éva Pócs has found the same ambiguity in Early Modern Hungary, and demonstrated how little separated the beliefs and activities of healers and 'witches' there. The distinction was often a matter of perspective alone, depending on agricultural and other rivalries between communities or neighbours, so that more than half of those brought to trial for witchcraft in Hungary were healers.[123] One man's healer or diviner is another man's witch.

Can we then say that cunning folk were witches? Again, Hutton's failure to define the terms 'witch' or 'witchcraft' makes it difficult to argue this with him. Outside of Neopagan witchcraft he only ever applies these terms to groups which have long been considered fictitious: the highly organised anti-Christian pagan resistance movement postulated by Margaret Murray or Jules Michelet, for instance, or the diabolised stereotype of grand witches' sabbats from the height of the European witch trials.[124] Should we then expect that any less grandiose form of cult will qualify for him as 'witchcraft'? That Hutton gives these tired old myths another good thrashing is fine, but I would also like to hear about the *real* history of witchcraft. Those fantasies of Murray, Michelet and the rest are little more than straw dolls nowadays, and to venture beyond them would have been a far greater triumph, for Hutton would then have had to look beyond popular literature, and make a far more time-consuming search through trial records, folklore and historical anthropology

---

[120] Macfarlane 1970 127.

[121] Hutton 1999a 106.

[122] Wilby 2005 123.

[123] Pócs 1999 12, 68–9, 88, 113, 124. David Lederer's findings in Bavaria are similar:

> magic, or what the authorities defined as witchcraft, sorcery, and superstition, was most certainly practised by real persons and was much more common than has been generally accepted by most historians. These practices were not just dreamed up by misogynous clergymen in spare moments of sexual frustration. Even if the vast majority of the accused in witch trials were not involved in diabolism (rare but extant devil's pacts indicate that some people surely were), many practised beneficent "white" magic. (Lederer 2002 52)

[124] I remain to be convinced that something along the lines of a 'grand sabbat' was not celebrated by the Basque people; I have heard accounts of such meetings of their native *Sorginak* religion within living memory.

to determine what actual folk magicians such as the British cunning women and men practised and believed.

Cranks and dilettantes

The modern world of witchcraft and occultism has more than its fair share of flakes and hucksters, whom Hutton enthusiastically exposes — in some cases a little too enthusiastically. Margaret Murray, for instance, was uncritical in projecting her own ideas into her research, and far too eager to derive vast generalisations from isolated instances, but Hutton's charge that she knowingly and wilfully distorted her evidence has been shown to itself rely on distortions and misquotations.[125] Similarly, when discussing the infamously inflated figure of nine million witchcraft executions throughout Europe, his charge that Matilda Joslyn Gage was a fraud who simply invented the figure is incorrect: an antiquarian in Quedlinburg, Germany came up with this estimate by extrapolating from local records, and several German and English historians, including Gage, repeated it.[126] But Hutton's brush is never short on tar, and

---

[125] Including some uncritically repeated from Norman Cohn; we shall touch again on this later. (Farrell-Roberts 2003a, 2003b; Don Frew 1998)

[126] Poole 2003 192. Earlier, in *Pagan Religions*, Hutton claimed that Gerald Gardner's associate Cecil Williamson had invented this figure (Hutton 1991 370). When writing *Triumph* he obviously realised his mistake and instead laid the blame on Gage, perhaps assuming that she was Williamson's immediate source (Hutton 1999a 141). He has since corrected his story (2003a 30). Hutton advanced his own estimate of 40,000 casualties of the witch-trials: this cuts a third off the previous lowest estimate (Hutton 1999a 132; 1991 306). His approach was to count estimated deaths by region, and extrapolate a figure for uncounted areas by matching that region with another of similar population, culture and apparent intensity of witch-hunting (Gibbons 1998).

Pagan historian Max Dashu is sceptical of Hutton's figure, and points out that an adequate estimate cannot easily be derived from existing records by statistical extrapolation. For a start, the records we have for most regions are very sporadic and only begin partway through the hunts, if they were kept at all. And these surviving records may be a poor guide to patching up the massive systemic gaps that remain, since evidence suggests that records tended to dry up especially during the heaviest waves of trials. There are a number of reasons for this, such as when regional courts and freelance witch-finders pursued unofficial hunts in defiance of state or church authorities. Even in regions where it was previously thought that records were fairly complete, chance discoveries of parallel sources have doubled prior estimates. Dashu observes that historians "have a tendency to be ruled by the nature of available documentation, which in this case is demonstrably flawed and incomplete". She also reminds us that estimates such as Hutton's do not include the many victims of earlier mediæval trials, nor do they count those who were not killed but

in his zeal he thoroughly blackens the faces of some who may deserve better.

One of those more severely castigated is Charles Leland. In the last years of the nineteenth century Leland published *Aradia, or the Gospel of the Witches*, containing a set of writings known as the *Vangel*, which he claimed were the collected lore of an Italian tradition of witchcraft. Leland was by all accounts a fabulously resourceful folk researcher, who managed to win the confidence and respect of Canadian Algonquins and English gypsies, and wrote pioneering works on their cultures and languages.[127] His *Etruscan-Roman Remains*, written prior to *Aradia*, has been confirmed as a rare, genuine record of the folklore of the Emilia-Romagna region.[128]

There is no single criticism of weight that Hutton can lay against Leland, but through a series of pedantic attacks on his scholarship he manages to paint him as a crank, a dilettante, a polemical anti-Catholic and a likely forger. For instance, Hutton complains of Leland's lack of evidence in stating that the Church's rituals and saints are often of pagan origin; but this was and still is a commonly accepted fact, for which Hutton need look no further than Keith Thomas' *Religion and the Decline of Magic* or a number of other books he has repeatedly cited.[129] As mentioned earlier, Hutton criticises Leland for using the word 'witch' instead of the specialised, Anglo-centric term 'cunning-man' or 'cunning-woman'. He also objects to Leland's supposedly romanticised depiction of the region his material was collected in, but seems to have misunderstood where this region was.[130] When Leland states that Aradia is the name of a pagan goddess, supposedly without providing evidence (in fact he does[131]), Hutton triumphantly interjects that this is clearly Herodias, a figure from Christian tradition (for which assertion Hutton himself supplies no evidence). In fact, Hutton should be well acquainted with Herodias or Aradia and her connection with witchcraft, as she appears in several of the works he claims to be familiar with.[132] Apparently "no other modern Italian folklorist has turned up evidence for anything

---

were "drowned, beaten, attacked and 'scored' (cut to draw blood), fined, imprisoned, exiled, shunned, expropriated or deprived of their livelihoods" (Dashu 1999). In Hutton's defence, another Pagan historian, Jenny Gibbons, believes he has properly accounted for skews in the available data (Gibbons 2000).

[127] Mathiesen 1998 25–9; Powell 1903.

[128] Pazzaglini 1998b 109.

[129] Thomas 1997 47–8. The assimilation of pagan ritual, deities and places of worship to Christianity is discussed further in a later chapter.

[130] Hutton 1999a 143–4. Toscana Romagna is (as Leland says) a remote, mountainous district straddling the provinces of Forli-Cesena and Ravenna, not a busy coastal plain! Pazzaglini's description of similar regions in northern Italy (isolated, with obscure dialects and unorthodox syncretisms of Christianity and fairy lore, as well as active traditions of folk magic) accords perfectly with Leland's account (Pazzaglini 1998a 93–8).

[131] Leland clearly cites Pipernus as the source of this assertion (Leland 1899 103). He also discusses his own reasoning for this identification at length in *Etruscan Roman Remains* (1892 150–153).

[132] Such as Cohn 1975 212; Rose 2003 113; Ginzburg 1990 90; Russell 1972 75; etc..

like the *Vangel*"[133] — what about the eminent Italian scholar Carlo Ginzburg (whose book *Ecstasies* Hutton later purports to critique), who has both provided ample evidence for the pagan origins of the name Aradia and catalogued long-standing traditions of witchcraft-like beliefs in this same area of Italy?[134] Has Hutton even read Ginzburg?[135] A careful reading of the following page reveals Hutton's implicit admission that Aradia is indeed recorded as a mythical figure in popular belief, possibly as early as the thirteenth century:

> . . . medieval Italy possessed ecclesiastical surveillance systems which allowed an inquisitor writing in the 1260s to publish detailed information on almost fifty varieties of heretical sect existing in the peninsula at that time; . . . but neither this nor any similar work ever mentions followers of Diana or Aradia, save as mythical figures in popular belief.[136]

Surely this was worth mentioning while he was rebuking Leland, claiming there was no evidence for the former existence of the deity. And of course the "ecclesiastical surveillance systems" in Italy *were* aware of these heretical beliefs from at least the ninth or tenth century, and documented them in over fifty inquisitorial trials and other works, which is how we know of them today.[137]

---

[133] Hutton 1999a 145.

[134] Ginzburg 1990 part 2, ch. 1. This 'Herodias' originates not in the biblical figure, but in *Hera-Diana* or *Herodiana*, whose name became normalised by baffled Christian writers to *Herodias*, a name which also neatly fit a negative Christian interpretation (p. 104). As Hutton notes, Aradia is an Italian variant of this name.

Diana appears again and again throughout the Christian period as a goddess receiving veneration, but it is unclear to which deity this name originally refers, or even if it is the same single deity, since Latin writers had a tendency to normalise any unfamiliar-sounding woodland goddess to this name. 'Diana' shows up in north Italy in the 380s, Spain in the late sixth century, Gaul in the late sixth and late seventh centuries (perhaps an assimilation of the Gaulish Arduinna, here), Germany in the 880s, the Rhinish Palatinate in the eleventh century, in the records of French and German church councils of 1280 and 1310, northern Italy in 1390, and so on into the height of the witch-trials. Ramsey MacMullen likens her to a dolphin in a distant school, seen only when it unexpectedly surfaces: "Is that, the observer wonders, the same dolphin's back each time, or some other?" (MacMullen 1997 74–5 and notes; Ginzburg 1990 90–92)

[135] I would guess he *hasn't* read Ginzburg's work, which he mischaracterises most wildly in a retort to Pagan historian Don Frew (Hutton 2000). Here Hutton insists that Ginzburg discussed witchcraft accusations only in "one district of Italy" (actually large sections of Europe) and never proposed that 'pagan survivals' featured in the beliefs and practices of the accused (this is actually the entire thrust of Ginzburg's *Ecstasies*). Ironically, this comes directly after Hutton's insinuation that Frew is unfit to comment on witchcraft history, since he "has apparently read not a single one" of Hutton's favourite books on the subject.

[136] Hutton 1999a 146.

[137] "Writing about 936, Rather, bishop of Liege and then of Verona, condemns those who believe that Herodias rules one-third of the world. This is the earliest mention of Herodias as a leader of evil spirits

Hutton's final *coup de grâce* is to quote from Leland's obituary, in which a friend of his says that

> ... he could and did make careful and exact notes, but when he put his results before the public he liked to give them the seal of his own personality and to allow his fancy to play about the stories and poems he was publishing[138]

Hutton presents this as a "damning admission" of Leland's dishonesty by a close friend; however that is not what is conveyed if the quotation is read in its original context. The original wording continues as follows:

> ..., so that those who were not able quickly to distinguish what was folklore and what was Leland were shocked, and grumbled (much to his astonishment and even disgust) and belittled his real achievements. He thought clearly, and many of his "guesses" have been or are being confirmed.[139]

Indeed, the process of confirmation continues. A critical edition of *Aradia*[140] published in the previous year to *Triumph* contains a new translation and detailed analyses of the book, including a scholarly essay by Robert Mathiesen examining the origins of the text. Mathiesen concludes that in all likelihood Leland received all his information in good faith, and that the text is authentic, although rather than being representative of a widespread tradition it is more likely a selection and adaptation of a single family's lore. Leland's transcription from the original manuscript still exists, and it appears that he misunderstood some of the dialect Italian and introduced minor errors into the translation.[141] This in itself would, it seems, substantially clear Leland of doubt.

---

of persons, and though Rather explicitly identifies her with the murderess of John the Baptist, he may unwittingly have been accepting a popular transformation of the unfamiliar name of Hecate into a Biblical name known to every Christian." (Russell 1972 75; as we have seen, Ginzburg differs on the derivation of the name.) According to Julio Caro Baroja, there is an even earlier mention of Herodias, identified with Diana, leading a host of women riding through the air on beasts. This is found in a few sources, including amongst legal fragments of Charles the Bald from 872 (Baroja 1968 60–61). Folklorist Jacob Grimm devotes a large section of Chapter 13 of his *Teutonic Mythology* to Herodias, and connects her very plausibly with pagan deities (Grimm 1998).

I arrived at the very conservative figure of fifty inquisitorial trials by adding up just the trials mentioned by Ginzburg (1990 9, 89, 91–2, 94).

[138] Hutton 1999a 147.

[139] Powell 1903. Powell further describes him as "full of life and energy and observation", "his memory exact and trustworthy", "a man of science, an observer, a recorder"; and numbers him among those who "seek incessantly and without pretence the far-off shrine of Truth".

[140] Leland 1998.

[141] Mathiesen 1998 39, 50.

We have now examined each one of Hutton's accusations against Leland, and they have all come to naught. Even so, we should not unquestioningly accept the *Vangel* as genuine. It is still possible that Leland's informant Maddelena wrote it, or even that he put her up to it; there are many ways the text could have originated and changed. Yet it warrants more serious attention than Hutton has given it. Indeed, comparing it with the traditions catalogued by Ginzburg should pique our interest, for we find that from the thirteenth century or earlier men and women in northern Italy and Sicily followed a goddess, believing that they left their bodies in spirit and congregated at great feasts presided over by her, where they were taught magic and divination; or that they flew into the clouds where they fought evil spirits to secure the fertility of the land. Their goddess was variously called Herodias (*Erodiade* in the vernacular), Richella, Herodiana and Abundia. The Friuli district near where Leland collected his material has come under particular scrutiny from witchcraft historians since the late 1960s, when Ginzburg discovered records of one such magical tradition: that of the Early Modern men and women who called themselves *benandanti*, or 'good-walkers'. This was a tremendously exciting discovery, since many scholars saw this as the most compelling evidence to date of an actual historical society of witches.[142] We do not know whether the *benandanti* followed other Italian shamanist traditions in naming their goddess Herodias, Diana, Richella or Abundia. The only record we have of her simply calls her "the abbess".[143]

Recently, Sabina Magliocco has discovered a divinity of similar name in Sardinia, a country with close ties to Italy since the twelfth century. Here Araja or Arada was patroness of the *janas* or fairies, and (under the name Erode) leader of the procession of the dead around All Hallows. She has survived as Sa Rejusta (*s'Araja justa*, 'the just Arada') or 'mama Erodas', a bogey linked with witchcraft beliefs, who snatches children if food is not left out for her, or who enters homes through the keyhole to check that unmarried girls have been studious with their housework and spinning. This almost precisely parallels the Germanic figure Frau Holda.[144]

We also find interesting parallels to Leland's material in Romania, a country with strong cultural ties to Italy.[145] There the goddess' name was Irodeasa or Arada (since, like the Early Modern Italians, they dropped the initial aspirate from 'Herodias'), or Doamna Zînelor 'Mistress of the Fairies'.[146] 'Saint' Irodeasa is still honoured there as the patron saint of the *călușari*, a surviving magical dance society who have remark-

---

[142] J. B. Russell called the *benandanti* "the most solid proof that was ever furnished regarding the existence of witchcraft", and Midelfort called them "the single witch cult documented to this day in Europe during the first centuries of the modern age". (Ginzburg 1990 10)

[143] "... a certain woman called the abbess, seated in majesty on the edge of a well" (Ginzburg 1983 54).

[144] Magliocco 2009.

[145] Kligman 1977 45.

[146] Ginzburg 1990 189.

able similarities to the *benandanti*.[147] We also find possible echoes of the *Vangel*'s cosmogony in Romanian folklore: in one tale the Sun attempts to wed his sister the Moon, Ileana Sânziana ('Fairy Saint-Diana'), just as in the *Vangel* Diana (the moon)

---

[147] The similarities between the two traditions extend even to seemingly minor points of detail; they are too numerous to list here, but one example may illustrate the kind of parallels we find: both *benandanti* and *căluşari*, when in combat against spirits or a rival group, are inextricably tied up with the fate of their flag-pole which must stay upright at all costs. If it should dip, one of their number will fall. (Ginzburg 1990 167; Kligman 1977 9, 32)

In his 2001 book *Shamans* Hutton revisits Ginzburg's work on the *benandanti*, and dismisses any connection between them and Siberian shamans on the basis of superficial differences, such as that the *benandanti* conducted their spirit-flights in private while shamans induce theirs in public (2001 144–6). Ginzburg, however, is pursuing deeper resemblances: he has identified a cluster of peculiar images and themes repeated with remarkable consistency across southern and central Europe over large time periods, and he seeks to discover their origins. The themes are often very specific, and include: the gathering and re-arranging of skin and bones of slain animals to aid their resurrection; being marked from birth for magic by a caul; patronage by a semi-bestial 'mother of the animals'; and asymmetry of beings who pass between worlds, often marked by a leg injury, misshapen foot or missing shoe. (Ginzburg 1990 134, 136, 171, 211, 214–6, 226–248) Several of these themes also reappear in rituals and myths of the European far north, central Siberia and even China and northern Japan, and Ginzburg hypothesises a very ancient diffusion from a central-Eurasian origin. That European magical practices have since evolved along somewhat different lines to Siberian shamanism is neither here nor there.

In *Shamans* Hutton also makes brief reference to young Romanian men who "supplied parades and entertainments under the patronage of a mythical empress 'Irodeasa'." (2001 146) These are of course the *căluşari*, who by Hutton's own criteria parallel shamans far more closely than any of the other European groups he discusses in detail (and dismisses). They were initiated in secrecy; had magic powers; flew from their bodies and communicated with spirits; performed public healing rituals involving trance and possession as well as improvisation and audience participation; could also curse; employed ritual clothing and tools; and fought both evil spirits and opposing *căluşari* from neighbouring communities (Kligman 1977). But it is not these broad parallels that Ginzburg finds pursuasive:

> . . . the suggestion that the dances and seasonal ceremonies [of *căluşari* and similar groups] should be seen as a derivation from shamanistic rituals, on the basis of elements like the use of the stick with the horse's head (hobby horse), seems insufficiently founded. (Ginzburg 1990 195)

Hutton makes a similarly superficial comparison between the Siberian shaman and the diabolised stereotype of the 'witch', and unsurprisingly finds more differences than similarities (2001 141–3). This observation reinforces his distancing of witchcraft from any real form of spiritual practice or belief. But the diabolical witch is a motif heavily encrusted with Christian theological impositions, and only dimly reflects the actual folk beliefs and practices of those accused of witchcraft. Peel these encrustations aside (following the lead of Ginzburg, Pócs and others), and the differences start looking more like similarities: competition and battles between white and black shamans (or between shamans of neighbouring communities) mirror the European battles and duels against evil spirits or sorcerers of neighbouring communities; the ambivalence between healing and cursing in Siberia mirrors the ambiguity between beneficent healer/diviner and malevolent witch; and the superhuman female 'witches' of Buryat mythology mirror the female fairies and non-human spirits that European magicians fought with, interacted with, and sometimes seemed (at least in part) to merge with. (See also Hutton 2001 77–8 regarding rivalries, duels and spirit-battles between shamans.) This doesn't make the accused witches shamans, but it does show that different cultures could share remarkably similar understandings of the magical world.

attempts to seduce her unwilling brother the sun.[148] Sânziana is described as a beautiful fairy, and gives her name to the festival of Midsummer, *Sânzienelor*, on which night the fairies, the *sânzienele*, gather to dance in the forest, where they imbue certain plants with magical properties and make predictions for unwedded girls. This festival used to be an important occasion for young people to meet and dance in the countryside, and many marriages were arranged.[149] This all sounds remarkably like the festivals described in *Aradia*. If *Aradia* is a forgery, its author has engaged with existing folklore with far greater sophistication than Hutton credits.

---

[148] Beza 1928 17, 19. For pointing out this connection I am indebted to Carla O'Harris, a superb folklorist and historian who has given me much help and encouragement.

[149] Marculescu; Ghinoiu. Compare also with the East Slavic spring festival *Rusal'naia nedelia* ('mermaid week') (Rappoport 1999).

Magic and ceremony

In Chapter 5, Hutton provides an extensive history of magic in Europe since the twelfth century — a difficult subject, as he himself acknowledges.[150] Although he mostly succeeds at this task, some oversights and inaccuracies are worth pointing out: magic's central importance to witchcraft demands that it receive careful treatment here. Broadly speaking, Hutton's account gives undue emphasis to radical innovation and discontinuity in the European magical tradition, making certain ideas and developments seem like bold new inventions when they are actually the end-point of a process of evolution.[151] This leads him to overstate the novelty of late nineteenth-century approaches to ceremonial magic, and even more so the novelty of Wicca's doctrines and techniques — all of which lends itself to his claim that most of these doctrines and techniques are unprecedented in earlier magic or religion.

Hutton uses the symbol of the pentagram, now synonymous with the occult, as a case study to show how major departures and innovations have repeatedly changed the face of European magic. For me, this same symbol offers a case study of the kinds of continuity Hutton has overlooked. To begin with, he tells us the symbol gained its enduring magical connotations (in an "interplay between scripture, divine harmony and mathematics") during the twelfth-century Renaissance, prior to which

---

[150] Magic "has its own language, logic, and conceptual structures, demanding a training equivalent to that of music and mathematics and proportionately different for a newcomer to comprehend" (Hutton 1999a 69).

[151] Ritual magicians in all ages have been natural antiquarians, more prone to collecting and preserving the ancient and the obscure than radically reinventing. Innovations, where they occur, are most often aimed at harmonising disparate pieces of material to develop a more workable system. There is a common belief amongst magicians that all divinely-inspired traditions flow from the same ultimate source and refer to the same universal truths, implying that a common system underlies them all and waits to be discovered. As occult historian Adam McLean puts it, "Magical or Hermetic thinking is the ability to see ideas as part of a whole — to see the interconnections, the correspondences, between seemingly diverse events, things and ideas." (McLean 1994 14). A more sceptical interpretation might be that superstitious minds tend to invest every charm with potency and every old and obscure text with hoary authority — and then seek to rationalise the resulting mish-mash.

there was no uniform tradition.[152] He is at least a thousand years out, for it already had famous and long-standing associations with divine harmony and mathematics, reputedly first applied by ancient Pythagoreans, and certainly in circulation by late antiquity.[153] Outside of that tradition the device has indeed been used for apparently mundane purposes such as potters' marks (as much today as in the ancient past), but it also has a long history as a mystical and apotropaic symbol in Persian, Hebrew and Greek magic.[154] It would seem, then, that the only major twelfth-century addition was the scriptural element. Later, in the nineteenth century, Hutton credits Eliphas Levi with being first to distinguish between an upright 'good' pentagram and an inverted 'evil' one, and first to 'trace' the pentagrams for invoking and banishing elemental forces at the four cardinal directions[155] — innovations, certainly, but perhaps not as groundbreaking as they first appear. The pentagram had long symbolised spirit (at the topmost point) in dominion over the four elements: not such a leap, then, to employ it in dominating and directing the elementals of the quarters.[156] Likewise an inverted pentagram, deposing spirit from its position of presidence, might well have been considered 'wrong' in some sense by any magician of the age. More innovative is Levi's system of tracing invoking or banishing pentagrams, starting at different points and proceeding in different directions depending on which element and whether invoking or banishing. But again, those sequences were largely suggested by the points' pre-existing elemental attributions — all that remained was to *trace* them.

By similar guesswork, Hutton attributes to W. B. Yeats the fusing of Christianity, Greco-Roman paganism and Qabalah in the symbol of the rose growing on the

---

[152] Hutton 1999a 67.

[153] The Pythagoreans, so Lucian tells us, invested it with both mystical and mathematical significance and called it ὑγίεια (*hygieia*), 'vitality, wholeness' (Sarton 1993 211). This tradition was taken up by Neopythagoreans of late antiquity, and again by Renaissance hermeticists such as Johann Heinrich Alstedius, Athanasius Kircher and Cornelius Agrippa.

[154] Luck 1986 55; Schouten 1968 19–28. By a possible coincidence, in the earliest Sumerian cuneiform inscriptions (c. 3000 BCE) the pentagram seems to represent 'regions', heavenly 'quarters' or 'directions', and is often found in conjunction with the number four. (Vogel 1966 292–3)

[155] Hutton 1999a 71. It is of course only supposition that Levi was author of these ideas. Levi was extremely well-connected and well-read in occultism, and could have relayed these ideas from sources now lost or obscure.

[156] Johann Reuchlin in 1494 applied the five letters of the Hebrew Pentagrammaton to the points of the Pythagorean pentagram, thus linking it with the name of Jesus and a rich set of elemental attributions still in use today (Idel 2008 53); he probably was not the first. And elemental associations with the four directions, the seasons, ages of man and so forth were already taking form as early as the writings of Ptolemy in the second century CE (Ashmand 1822 book 1 chapters 4–8, 10, 17; book 2 ch. 3).

Also, diagrams of magic circles from the grimoire tradition often included four pentagrams defensively drawn around them — though these were normally placed at the cross-quarters rather than the cardinal directions.

Tree of Life, as if this were Yeats' innovation.[157] This is actually the famous symbol of the Rose-Cross, connected by mystics with the Tree of Life.[158] The inner order of the Golden Dawn, the Rosæ Rubeæ et Aureæ Crucis (of which Yeats was a member), had as its identifying badge the Rose Cross Lamen, a symbol which permuted the Qabalistic Tree of Life and its twenty-two paths into the form of a cross with a central rose of twenty-two petals.

Hutton has repeatedly insisted that magic and religion are two distinct phenomena traditionally falling into different spheres, and that the blending of the two found in modern magic and witchcraft is thus a remarkable departure from any past mode of worship.[159] Wiccan scholar Don Frew challenged this, pointing out that systems such as late Classical theurgy (a type of ritual magic) could involve "most of the blurring of religion and magic that is so typical of modern Craft. Hutton's blanket statement that no pagan of antiquity would ever do this simply isn't true."[160] Yet Hutton still maintains that religion deals with forces outside human control, while magic seeks to compel and manipulate these forces: the priest requests; the magician demands.[161] But the kind of god-bullying that Hutton describes is only one approach to

---

[157] "Yeats' own aim was to fuse Christian and pre-Christian traditions as equivalent fulfilments of the some [sic] human needs: 'Because the Rose, the flower sacred to the Virgin Mary, and the flower that Apuleius's adventurer ate, when he was changed out of the ass's shape and received into the fellowship of Isis, is the western Flower of Life, I have imagined it growing upon the Tree of Life'. In one sentence there, he had fused Christianity, Graeco-Roman paganism, and the cabbala." (Hutton 1999a 157)

[158] For example, Rudolf Steiner (1998 31).

[159] He first argued this in *Pagan Religions*: "Historians, theologians and anthropologists seem to be in general agreement upon the distinction between the two"; and, "Whether courtly or rural, learned or traditional, benign or malignant, it [magic] was an art or a science, not part of a religion." "It would have been inconceivable to any ancient European pagan of whose thought we have evidence, that the purpose of religious ritual was to 'raise' a deity and 'work' with her or him." (Hutton 1991 289–291, 335)

[160] Frew 1998. Other aspects of this exchange between Frew and Hutton are detailed below. P. G. Maxwell-Stuart, as we have already seen, seems to side with Hutton in treating magic as separate from religion; however, other historians such as Ginzburg have demonstrated how spiritually significant magical practices could be for some people. Ramsey MacMullen sums up the field in general:

> ... even a generation ago, it would have required considerable discussion: namely, the relationship between magic and religion and the exact meaning of the two terms. For historians of the West, knowing only their own discipline and only the one Judeo-Christian religious tradition, these matters used to be intellectually as well as theologically indigestible. Now, the lessons of anthropology grown familiar, it is common to accept the impossibility of separating magic from religion and to move on to more interesting subjects. (MacMullen 1997 143–4)

In the endnote to this MacMullen chronicles this shift in academic understanding among historians and anthropologists, which began in the mid 1970s.

Pagan researcher Jenny Gibbons observes that the word 'magic' likely originated as a derogatory label for the religions of others: supernatural power that was seen as suspicious, bad or inferior, as opposed to the supernatural power of one's own 'true' religion (Gibbons 2000).

[161] Hutton 1999a 394. Elsewhere he forgets himself and says that the "irrational qualities in religion"

magic, and more commonly-encountered approaches have little to distinguish them from religion. Consider that in many Christian denominations priests are afforded certain infallible powers such as the ability to perform transubstantiation. This sacrament is held to be effective *ex opere operato*; that is, it depends only on the prescribed actions being performed and the priest's intention to perform them. Even if he performs them poorly or is in a state of sin, the formula is assured of success. What difference, then, when a mediæval magician performs his own arcane ritual calling on the names of God to help him bind spirits to his will? In neither case is deity being coerced, even though a human seemingly initiates the action. Jesus is not *forced* into the wine and wafers; Tetragrammaton Tzabaoth is not *forced* to constrain spirits; both rituals are held to work by the grace of God, through the intercession of a human operator.[162] And magic need not carry an assurance of success: the Greco-Egyptian triple-goddess invocation, the Old English Earth Mother invocation and the *Æcerbot* ritual (all previously mentioned) are little more than dressed-up and ritualised prayer, with no implication of being automatically effective.

By Hutton's account, magic ceased being a purely coercive tool only in the late nineteenth century, largely due to the innovation of the Hermetic Order of the Golden Dawn, which turned it into a means for personal development. He tells us that the overpowering and subjugation of demons in earlier grimoires such as the *Abramelin* rite is "an elaborate way of ringing for room service", very different to the newer Golden Dawn style of magic that was concerned with human progress and improvement.[163] There are several problems in this brief statement. For a start, the Golden Dawn did in fact deal with demons, which they understood to reside partially in the magician's own psyche, as destructive aspects of the magician's self;[164] one aspect of the 'Great Work' of a Golden Dawn magician was to overpower these demons and turn them to a useful purpose: "Nature persuadeth us that there are pure daemons and that even the evil germs of Matter may alike become useful and good."[165] The *Abramelin* rite, on the other hand, was well regarded within the Golden Dawn, presumably because it accorded so well with the teachings of the Order; it was

---

such as faith-healing, speaking in tongues or possession by demons or the Holy Spirit "can be called magical" (p. 405).

[162] Our magician still coerces *spirits*, of course, as does a Christian exorcist.

[163] Hutton 1999a 82.

[164] It is widely held among modern occultists that the mediæval grimoires were written under the same understanding, i.e., that the spirits were (at least in part) elements of the magician's own mind (King 1975 12; Snell 1979 33).

[165] From the Practicus grade ritual of the Golden Dawn (Regardie 1989 171; vol. II 101 in original edition). A candidate in the Adeptus Minor grade ritual symbolically treads down their personal demons (Regardie 1989 243; vol. II 238 in original edition), and in the consecration ceremony for a Jupiter talisman the "legions of demons who dwell in the land of twilight" are called to serve the operator as their master (Regardie 1989 419; vol. III 221–2 in original edition).

first translated into English by the Order's co-founder, S. L. MacGregor Mathers. It seems that few members practised it though — it was and is notorious as one of the most harrowing magical operations in the Western tradition, requiring unbroken discipline over the course of six months to safely complete it — a far cry from "room service"![166]

While allowing that modern magic is no longer purely coercive, Hutton still distances it from other types of religious expression. He tells us, for instance, that 'worship' in any normal sense was not written into Golden Dawn rituals: "it was far from obvious, in the performance of the Qabalistic Cross, whether the kingdom, the power, and the glory belonged to God or were being promised to the human carrying out the ritual".[167] The real answer to this conundrum (as with so many other magical paradoxes) is that both are true. The entity addressed in this ritual is not the human self but the 'universal self' (i.e. God), of which all creatures and all creation are considered emanations or divided fragments. The magician believes that he or she shares in God's being, and aspires to harmonise his or her personal self as much as possible with the universal self — though final conscious union with God is only achieved at the loss of all individuality. Thus the Qabalistic Cross ritual affirms that man and God are ultimately one.[168] This and other Golden Dawn rituals are certainly a form of worship, though they little resemble the simple adoration of church worship, having more in common with Masonic worship or various types of asceticism. The focus is on active, continuous spiritual realisation so that the individual becomes a more potent agent of divine expression in the world. Similar approaches are found in numerous schools of mysticism.

Hutton isolates the magical practices of modern witches in other ways. The rites of Pagan witchcraft require discipline, concentration and control, we are told, and thus differ from many tribal and shamanist practices in which consciousness is aban-

---

[166] The Golden Dawn's real contribution was, I suggest, their complete systematisation of magic, combining and extending structures already established by Qabalah, Freemasonry and Theosophy, and magicians such as Edward Kelley, John Dee and Eliphas Levi. While relatively few of the Golden Dawn's ideas were new, the remarkably elegant synthesis they formed of these ideas was unprecedented, a cross-referencing of multiple systems that brought new illumination to them all.

[167] Hutton 1999a 79.

[168] In the same way, ascending the Tree of Life is, for a Hermetic Qabalist, a means of attuning and ultimately merging with God, not merely a way of gaining knowledge and power as Hutton describes (1999a 82). And this ascent is achieved not just through "contemplation", but through intense work on all levels from the physical to the spiritual. Hutton's very brief explanation of Qabalah falls short in other ways too: its structure is indeed built around "ten emanations of the One God", but these don't correspond to the Hebrew alphabet (which is instead applied to the twenty-two 'paths' of movement between these emanations), nor are the ten emanations normally combined into a "single great divine name" (perhaps he's thinking of the *Shemhamephorasch*, or 'Divided Name'?). Hermetic Qabalah forms the framework for almost the entirety of modern ceremonial magic, and is in turn a vast influence on Wicca, one not explored by Hutton.

doned to ecstasy and euphoria.[169] Exactly what he means by 'tribal' is unclear, but the distinction nonetheless seems misconceived. Wicca contains rites that are wild and orgiastic, just as 'tribal' rites include those that are rigid and formal. Perhaps the most celebrated of the 'tribal' magical religions is Vodou, which incorporates the rites of several African and Caribbean tribes. For some years I worked with a Mambo Asogwe who ran her *hounfor*, or temple, with the same strict discipline she had learnt in Haiti. Constant alertness was paramount, and participants were scolded if they withdrew into themselves or tried to 'go into a trance'. It is a common misconception that one must dull one's senses in order to enter an altered magical state, something that in my experience has never been the case in any system of working, even if the ultimate goal is ritual possession (whether by the Goddess, God or Vodou *Loa*).

Hutton has more recently claimed that Wicca's doctrine of reincarnation is not of British or European origin, but comes from Eastern philosophy that filtered into Britain from the eighteenth century.[170] Possibly so, but he is incorrect to state that the doctrine was previously unknown in Europe or Britain. The belief was held by numerous ancient Mediterranean philosophers, including Pythagoras, Plato, Apollonius of Tyana and Plotinus, and it continued in currency among the Gnostics. Julius Caesar recorded the belief among the Druids of Gaul and Britain, and there are suggestions of the same belief later among the Norse. Christian apologists such as Tertullian continued to fulminate against the doctrine of reincarnation in the first few centuries after Christ, which suggests that it was still commonplace; it blossomed again in the later Middle Ages — most famously amongst the thirteenth-century Cathars — and was treated as a dangerous heresy. The belief was promoted again in the Italian Renaissance by Pico della Mirandola and Giordano Bruno, and thereafter persisted in poetry and literature with numerous references and endorsements. In Britain reincarnation seems also to have persisted as a native belief long after the coming of Christianity: it was recorded among Celtic Scots, Welsh and Irish in 1911.[171]

---

[169] Hutton 1999a 407.

[170] "[Reincarnation] is not a Western idea at all, though confusion has been created among English-reading occultists by the American mystic Edgar Cayce, who declared that it was Christian doctrine until declared heresy by a sixth-century Council of Constantinople. This is post-Christian special pleading: the doctrine condemned at Constantinople was that God created each individual soul in advance, at the beginning of time, which is not the same thing as reincarnation. The concept of reincarnation comes from the East, being especially associated with Hindu and Buddhist thought. It reached Europe, like so much else, in the eighteenth century, and was especially influential in Britain because the British conquest of India, followed by Ceylon and Burma, opened a highway for it." (Hutton 2009b)

[171] Stevenson 2003 5–8. It is still unknown whether the Christian theologian Origen taught fully-fledged reincarnation or merely the pre-existence of souls, though Hutton asserts the latter, and Edgar Cayce the former. Shakespeare's references to Pythagoras and reincarnation in *Twelfth Night* 4:2, *As You Like It* 3:2 and *The Merchant of Venice* 4:1 were presumably understood by his audiences. (Stevenson 2003 7, 8)

Although Wicca is unique among religions and occult societies, most of its constituent elements are neither unprecedented nor even that uncommon in earlier religion and magic. Behind its trappings Wicca is quite similar to many other schools of mysticism, including historical ones such as Neoplatonism.

Hutton has also been misinformed regarding Freemasonry (and the particular branch that is Co-Freemasonry) on a matter crucial to his most damning accusation against Gerald Gardner: Gardner claimed to be a Royal Arch Freemason, but according to Hutton "the Royal Arch is the highest, most exclusive and most prestigious of all Masonic degrees",[172] so this claim is probably untrue. This accusation, that Gardner might invent a magical or ceremonial history for himself, puts a big question mark over his account of being initiated into Wicca. But this is all a misunderstanding: in some Masonic bodies the Royal Arch degree is indeed the furthest that a Mason can progress, but in constitutions that work the 'York Rite' or the 'Scottish Rite', such as Co-Freemasonry, there are numerous further degrees. I myself am a Royal Arch Mason in Co-Freemasonry, working the same rituals and same degree structure Gardner would have worked. Four or five years in Masonry is usually enough for someone to progress to Holy Royal Arch, if they are eager; and this process has been dramatically sped up on occasion for individuals who were considered especially qualified.

New research published by Philip Heselton shows that several of the likely members of the New Forest Coven, whom Gardner met through a Rosicrucian Theatre, were Co-Freemasons; furthermore, one of the principal members of the Theatre was Mabel Besant Scott, who had previously been the Grand Commander of the British Federation of Co-Freemasonry! (She, in fact, held the highest, thirty-third degree in Scottish Rite Freemasonry.)[173] So, given the interests of his friends and acquaintances, I would be surprised if a man of Gardner's leanings *hadn't* been a Co-Freemason and a member of the Holy Royal Arch.[174] He certainly would have been foolish to falsify this degree to Aleister Crowley, who could easily test him. Incidentally, it was Mabel Besant Scott's mother, Annie Besant, whom Hutton incorrectly names as the founder of Co-Freemasonry in the early twentieth century.[175] Annie Besant, the famous Theosophist, Liberal Catholic and Co-Mason helped spread Co-Freemasonry throughout the English-speaking world, but the movement was founded not by her but by Mlle. Maria Deraimes, Dr. Georges Martin and sixteen

---

[172] Hutton 1999a 219.

[173] Heselton 2000 94–6.

[174] Doreen Valiente affirms that both he and Dafo (Edith Woodford-Grimes) were Co-Masons (Valiente 2007 56); the records of *Harmony* Lodge No. 25 in Southampton, to which he most likely belonged, have unfortunately been destroyed, making absolute proof of this rather difficult (Heselton 2003 292).

[175] Hutton 1999a 58, 213.

other French Freemasons in Paris in 1893.[176]

---

[176] Mackey 1912 "Co-Masonry".

The elusive "Old Dorothy"

When Hutton turns to the task of establishing whether Dorothy Clutterbuck was truly involved with the New Forest coven, as Gardner had claimed to some of his initiates,[177] we are obliged to rely on Hutton's own interpretations of the data. This may be inescapable, since *Triumph* covers too much ground to provide extensive quotations. But can we rely on his interpretation to be fair?

Let's look at Dorothy's diary entries, about which Hutton simply states: "The woman they reveal is a simple, kindly, conventional, and pious one. Absolutely none of them — including those at the time of the four major witch festivals — have any relevance to paganism or the occult."[178] Philip Heselton has since provided a more detailed description of the diaries she kept, and even published quite a few entries from them, enabling us to check the accuracy of Hutton's evaluation.[179] The diaries paint her as a spiritual woman, but not in the conventional Church of England sense. They do indeed contain references to God and saints, but only three rather oblique mentions of Christ or Christianity.[180] Within the two years covered by the diaries, both Christmases are unconventionally personified as a female figure, a "Radiant Creature ... laughing as she goes. The shining holly fills her lap",[181] "her mantle made of Holly Leaves / Fringed round with Berries Red / And, her own Christmas Roses / Set like Stars around Her Head".[182] A radiant female being is a very frequent theme, appearing as a fairy-like dancing maiden, often referred to as 'the Queen', and per-

---

[177]'Old Dorothy' is one of the most enigmatic figures in the history of Wicca. Gerald Gardner claimed that his initiation into the New Forest Coven (as one of 'the Wica' [sic]) took place in her house, and for many years it was widely supposed that she was his initiator and High Priestess of the group; others assumed that both she and the coven were fabrications invented by Gardner to legitimise his new religion. Her existence since proven (Valiente 1984), Hutton now wonders if Dorothy truly was a witch, or an uninvolved party implicated by Gardner for his own inscrutable reasons.

[178]Hutton 1999a 211.

[179]Heselton 2000 156–176.

[180]Heselton 2000 162.

[181]Christmas 1942.

[182]Christmas 1943.

sonifying the seasons and the land. For example:

> The day I saw you dancing / In that gold October wood / I thought
> you were a fairy / In your little scarlet hood / I thought the swaying
> beeches / Made your floating golden hair / And that rose pink spindle
> berries / Had dyed your cheeks so fair . . . And then I thought "I'll go
> quite close / And look in to her eyes" / They were purple Autumn violets
> / And, at once, they made me wise / I knew you were a vision / The
> loveliest ever seen / But I also knew that you were Real / And of my
> heart, the Queen.[183]
>
> I am waiting for my Lady / For, down the pathway shadey / I think I
> hear her footfall light / My heart beats wildly with delight . . . / I cannot
> wait — the minutes drag / Just when I'm in despair / Dear Heaven! She
> is coming! And now She's here! She's here![184]

Nature and the feelings of magical enchantment that come from it fill the diaries;
there are also frequent references to fairies, bits of herb-lore, and occasional vivid
descriptions of Classical deities such as Aurora. The moon features regularly, and
is regarded in terms that would be familiar to Wiccans: "The deep Blue Sky, just
shot with Silver Gleam / Where, behind clouds, there rises the night's queen / Send-
ing Her Fairy Light across the flowers / Oh! what Enchantment lies / In these rare
Hours."[185]

Is this really the Church stalwart Hutton has portrayed? "Simple, kindly, conventional and pious"? True, witchcraft is never explicitly mentioned in the diaries,
but then, Dorothy intended them to be viewed by her visitors. I think their "relevance to paganism" is worth a more careful look.

We may possibly gain a further insight into them by comparing them with the
writings of Katherine Oldmeadow, who lived near Dorothy and was her best friend.
Dorothy always intended the diaries to be given to her, and she received them upon
Dorothy's death.[186] Oldmeadow was a children's author whose books demonstrate an
almost identical sensibility to Dorothy's diaries, with the same absence of Christian
themes, the same reverence for nature and belief in fairies and magic,[187] and the same

---

[183] 27 October 1943.

[184] 30 July 1942.

[185] 12 July 1943.

[186] Heselton 2003 34–63.

[187] "Doors are wonderful things. . . There is the Door into Fairyland — the most wonderful door of
all — which one seeks and never finds." (Oldmeadow commenting for herself, not one of her characters)
(Heselton 2003 41) "Jill never smiled as she made this speech, in fact she looked so solemn that Rory
hugged herself and Satan [a black Persian cat] with joy; for to be in a wood just after dawn with a girl
who made an offering to the fairies thrilled her imagination, as she really believed in the Little People as
firmly as did her old nurse, and to her every tree and flower in the Glen was haunted by the fairy folk."

fascination with Classical pagan deities, particularly Pan and the nymphs, whom her characters dress up as in the woods for their highly ritualised games. A girl takes the rôle of Pan,[188] while another female character is actually named 'Pan'. Another frequent theme is secret societies with elaborate initiation ceremonies and occult overtones.[189] Elsewhere we read of divination (one character is "fay" and can see the past, present and future reflected in glass) and magical objects such as witches' mirrors and witch-balls. Oldmeadow also wrote a non-fiction book, *The Folklore of Herbs*, in which she frequently refers to ancient pagan wisdom underlying the religious and magical uses of herbs;[190] she also discusses at length the distinction between white and black witchcraft, and affirms the current-day existence of white witches.[191]

Another likely acquaintance of Dorothy's was Rosamund Sabine, who was implicated in witchcraft and the New Forest coven in Gerald Gardner's and Doreen Valiente's private writings. (Gardner also served with Sabine's husband on the Highcliffe Local Defence Volunteers, which used one of Dorothy's houses for rest and recreation.) Sabine was apparently a long-standing Golden Dawn magician and a herbalist.[192] It seems then that Dorothy could easily have been exposed through her social circle to ideas surrounding paganism, secret societies, witchcraft and ceremonial magic.

That Gardner might have implicated Dorothy in witchcraft as a decoy or a prank is still possible, but perhaps a long shot, given that he never published her surname, even in part, but only mentioned it to a few initiates: it's hard to see what he could expect to gain through such an obscure misdirection.[193] Heselton has also pointed out that it was only ever an assumption that Dorothy was the leader of the New For-

---

(Heselton 2003 45)

[188] "'I'll be Pan,' announced Jill with determination. 'I don't care if he is a boy. I simply love him, and I'm like him, too, because I adore wandering over mountains and rocks and woods and having people dance round me and teasing them.' . . . her expression of almost fiendish merriment was the very Pan of one's imagination. She was half-draped in a goat-skin, and in her brown, slender fingers she held a flute of reeds." (Heselton 2003 46)

[189] One such society, the "Red Circle", is a "cult" based on numerology, its members limited to those children whose names reveal them to have been born in the element of Fire. Other societies in her stories involved writing one's name in blood, the teaching of "mystic signs" ("which were maddening to the uninitiated") and other ritualistic acts. (Heselton 2003 53–56)

[190] For instance, she names mullein as "one of the witches' herbs. . . under the dominion of Saturn", and asserts that Christian monks "left out the heathen rites and ceremonies connected with the picking of plants and substituted prayers and psalms" — "In spite of the efforts of the monks, however, it took centuries to put an end to pagan rites and stamp out certain superstitions." (Heselton 2003 49–51)

[191] For example, she states: "The white witch of today still holds queer beliefs about mixing creatures with her simple medicines, and only a short time ago a gypsy woman advised the author to take 'a strong cup of snail tea' for a bad cough." (Heselton 2003 60)

[192] Heselton 2003 64–78.

[193] The surname Gardner gave is also odd, because for the entire period of Gardner's retirement in England she was known publicly as Dorothy St. Quintin Fordham, not Clutterbuck (Heselton 2000 148).

est coven and Gardner's initiator; Gardner never stated this. Heselton proposes that while she was likely a wealthy member of the coven who lent her house for some of their ceremonies, the leader of the group and Gardner's initiator were probably two other women, Rosamund Sabine and Edith Woodford-Grimes respectively.[194] This hypothesis, supported by large quantities of new evidence, resolves all of the major faults Hutton finds with the story, apart from the inarguable fact that Dorothy was a member of the Anglican church. I see no contradiction in this, though, since plenty of Wiccans have also been Christian;[195] I had presumed she was the "occasional conformist" Christian witch whom Gardner mentions in *Witchcraft Today*.[196] Unlike the other charitable and political groups she put so much energy into, she seems to have had little involvement with any special Church activities, and was probably not a particularly enthusiastic or committed member.[197]

Despite numerous false starts, some of the evidence Hutton raises against Gardner is both valid and significant, such as Gardner's falsification of a Ph.D. (though the suggestion that he "always" styled himself 'Dr.' is misleading, since he normally never used this title himself, but didn't correct others if they used it of him[198]). Both Doreen Valiente and Frederic Lamond testify to Gardner's ability to deceive.[199] But Hutton's facts are so tangled up with his fallacies that I would look to Valiente instead for the most reliable account of the man. She worked closely with Gardner as his High Priestess, and knew more of his background, perhaps, than any other of his initiates. Despite her deep involvement she was no easy dupe, and seems to have been unafraid to challenge even her own fondest beliefs in pursuit of truth. The picture she paints of Gardner is of one who loved being the centre of attention and was sometimes naïve in his judgement, but was nonetheless a great man and a true devotee who strove to preserve the religion he had inherited.[200]

---

[194] Heselton 2003 ch. 3; Heselton 2000 ch. 9.

[195] According to Maxine Sanders, when she first came to the Craft many Wiccans were also practising Christians, some even holding significant lay positions in their church (Sanders 2008 51). I personally know three Wiccans who are ordained priests in different Christian denominations, and Christianity has also been a large demographic in the ceremonial, magical, Masonic and Rosicrucian orders I have worked with over the years.

[196] Gardner 2004 40.

[197] Heselton 2000 192–3.

[198] Hutton 1999a 207; Don Frew, cited in Magliocco 2004 240.

[199] Valiente 2007; Lamond 2004.

[200] Valiente 2007 65, 80.

Christian eclipse

In *Triumph*, Hutton's sympathy for modern Paganism is quite clear, despite many of his theories detracting from the traditional Pagan world-view. A lot of these theories are carried over from his earlier book *Pagan Religions of the Ancient British Isles*, which is worth extended consideration. In it, his sympathies are much less clear: his tone is withering, and he characterises Neopagans as "radical" and irrational. (He later admitted to another researcher that he had been angry when writing it; he saw Neopagans promoting false histories as the book's "natural opponents".[201]) Christianity, on the other hand, he positively eulogises, with turns of phrase that make 'providence' rather than chance determine victory for Constantine and the rising Christian empire, while pagans "brought catastrophe upon themselves".[202] He sides with the theory that Christianity brought significant changes for the good, emerging from its own intense persecution to extend greater tolerance to women and lower social ranks such as slaves, while also actively preserving pagan art, literature and temples. The case that Christianity might have been a step backward is, he confidently tells us, "thoroughly unacademic and embodied in works of fiction, tracts and radical periodicals rather than scholarly books".[203]

Six years after Hutton wrote this, Ramsey MacMullen, hailed by the American Historical Association as "the greatest historian of the Roman Empire alive today",[204] would press exactly that case. For a start, far from ending persecutions, Christian rule brought similar persecution against pagans, Jews and Manichees. Even

---

[201] Farrell-Roberts 2003a.

[202] Hutton 1991 248–9. In discussing Christianity's "near-incredible strokes of luck — or acts of providence" that "could readily be called miraculous", he repeats Christian myth, whereby (for example) Constantine's vision of a cross presaged an "amazingly fortunate victory" at the battle of Milvian Bridge. It's a nice story for Sunday school, but let's not forget that Constantine was a skilled general while Maxentius, with little or no military experience, had also just lost his senior general; of the two armies, though roughly even in size, Constantine's was far better trained (Bunson 1995 277–8; Rees 2002 156–7; Williams 1997 203).

[203] Hutton 1991 249–253.

[204] At their 2001 annual meeting, where he received the Award for Scholarly Distinction.

the persecution of Christians (through sectarian rivalries) increased to an all-time high.[205] Both women and slaves substantially lost privilege under Christianity,[206] and there was little outreach (or message of salvation) to the lower classes, who were instead threatened with eternal torment in Hell, it being held by church leaders that fear was most effective in convincing a crowd.[207] Pagan books (and books of 'heterodox' Christians) were burned in large public bonfires,[208] and marauding Christian monks and *parabalani* smashed idols, destroyed temples and terrorised the populace.[209] True, laws were enacted to preserve pagan sculptures and temples, but other laws expressly called for their destruction. Some temples, such as the mile-long Caelestis shrine in Carthage, required great armies of workers to level.[210]

Any legal tolerance initially afforded to pagans was gradually eroded, until by the reigns of Justinian, Tiberius and Mauricius in the sixth century the unbaptised were terrorised by threat of mutilation, beheading or being burned alive (or, ironically, crucifixion or being torn apart by wild animals), along with confiscation of all property. One persecution in Harran ordered by Mauricius resulted in many people being carved up and their limbs hung to festoon the main street. Despite this, Harran remained, into the eleventh century, one of the last bastions of open pagan worship and pagan learning,[211] while the majority of Europe plunged into the Dark Ages.

Actually, pagan worship continued for centuries elsewhere too, alongside Christianity, since so many of the baptised were beyond the reach of religious instruction:

---

[205] MacMullen 1997 14. "[I]n the century opened by the Peace of the Church, more Christians died for their faith at the hands of fellow Christians than had died before in all the persecutions".

[206] Women were forbidden to worship together, approach the altar, teach or preach; homiletics were almost entirely addressed to men's, not women's concerns, and women's prayers at saints' martyriums had to be offered through male intermediaries, since women could not enter. Under paganism priestesses had presided over entire provinces, city cults and larger or smaller cult groups (some for women-only); they were admitted into the full range of initiations and could lecture in public on religion or perform official functions at public events; female deities, too, had received just as much cult service as male. In terms of legal protection too women suffered: under paganism a man who killed a prostitute could be put to death while under Christianity in the same period women were beheaded for adultery. As to slaves, there is no hint that their suffering was reduced under Christian owners, though their religious freedoms were severely reduced: previously they "had free access to almost all cults and temples, they mixed promiscuously among most cult groups, and commonly formed their own cult groups with their own priests and officials"; now, they were barred from priesthood for fear that they would 'pollute' that office. (MacMullen 1997 7–8)

[207] MacMullen 1997 10–11.

[208] MacMullen 1997 4–5. Also, copyists were threatened with having their hands cut off if they attempted to replace them.

[209] MacMullen 1997 11–17. The violence and lawlessness of these 'shock troops' was a major headache to civil authorities — even their bishops seemed unable to control them.

[210] MacMullen 1997 52–3.

[211] MacMullen 1997 20–31. We shall return briefly to Harran in the next chapter.

"they were poor and rural and hard to get at, rarely to be seen in church. Yet they counted in the tens of millions." Christian farmers and shepherds of the Euphrates, for instance, explained to a visiting anchorite that they hadn't seen a priest in living memory, and had forgotten everything they or their ancestors knew of Christianity. For some, conversion had been only nominal and they remained pagan by conviction.[212] Even those who were truly converted held so strongly to their past modes of worship that Christianity was forced to shape itself around their pagan impulses. The Marian cult, the martyr cult, saints as interlocutors, ritual offerings, most festival customs, and a plethora of other activities such as dancing, singing and temple sleeps — all were transposed from paganism, as necessities of the popular religious psyche that the church was otherwise unable to provide. Despite their inconsistency with traditional doctrine, many of these innovations received hesitant (or enthusiastic) support from church leaders.[213] One of the greatest innovators was surely Constantine himself, who seems to have been aware he was not so much conforming to an existing religion as inventing a new one according to his own whims. Witness his comment: "We have received from Divine Providence the supreme favor of being relieved from all error".[214]

Hutton does not acknowledge this great influence paganism has had on Christianity. On the contrary, he is dismissive of the theories of Edward Clodd and Walter Johnson, two of the first scholars to suggest that many churches rest upon pagan holy sites, and that the rituals and myths of Christianity were often assimilations from previous non-Christian religion.[215] In *Triumph* he concludes that these theories "have not been borne out by investigation", despite some churches showing traces of pre-Christian activity.[216] We still have the letter sent by Pope Gregory the Great to Abbot Mellitus in 601, four years after Augustine's arrival in England:

---

[212] MacMullen 1997 144–6.

[213] MacMullen 1997 ch. 4.

[214] MacMullen 1997 130.

[215] Hutton 1999a 121–2. He even suggests in *Pagan Religions* that Knowlton Church was constructed inside the henge there for no other reason than that the henge provided a convenient churchyard and a bit of temporary shelter. (Hutton 1991 288)

[216] Hutton 1999a 122. Does absence of evidence equate to evidence of absence? Hutton himself admits that pagan activities need not have left archaeological traces. That such traces have survived at even a minority of sites is therefore an important fact not to be glossed over. Alain Dierkens explains why so few pagan remains have been found beneath churches (he's discussing Merovingian churches, but similar arguments presumably apply to British ones): in almost every case, small churches and their archaeological treasures were obliterated as larger churches replaced them; and even when occasional interesting finds are made during restoration or the installation of central heating, conditions are rarely conducive to proper scientific investigation. Nonetheless, the few excavations carried out under favourable conditions "have often yielded proof of continuity between the pagan and Christian phases", a symptom of the "deliberate policy of recycling pagan places of worship to serve the new religion." (Dierkens 1998 41)

... .tell [Bishop Augustine] what I have decided after long deliberation about the English people, namely that the idol temples of that race should by no means be destroyed, but only the idols in them. Take holy water and sprinkle it in these shrines, build altars and place relics in them. For if the shrines are well built, it is essential that they should be changed from the worship of devils to the service of the true God... And because [this people] are in the habit of slaughtering much cattle as sacrifices to the devils, some solemnity ought to be given them in exchange for this. So on the day of the dedication or the festivals of the holy martyrs, whose relics are deposited there, ... let them celebrate the solemnity with religious feasts[217]

Regarding pagan practices in general, historian Keith Thomas tells us of

the notorious readiness of the early Christian leaders to assimilate elements of the old paganism into their own religious practice, rather than pose too direct a conflict of loyalties in the minds of new converts. The ancient worship of wells, trees and stones was not so much abolished as modified, by turning pagan sites into Christian ones and associating them with a saint rather than a heathen divinity. The pagan festivals were similarly incorporated into the Church year. ... The hundreds of magical springs which dotted the country became 'holy wells', associated with a saint, but they were still employed for magical healing and for divining the future.[218]

Of the various ritual customs retained, such as well-dressing or May Day fires, "Some were customary calendar rituals whose pagan origins had long been forgotten, whereas others retained a frankly magical purpose."[219] Historians like Thomas are thus very much at odds with Hutton regarding residual pagan survivals, and paganism's influence on Christianity.[220]

The foliate heads (or 'Green Man' carvings) found in churches have long been interpreted as relics of paganism. Hutton states in *Pagan Religions* that a connection

---

[217] Kaspersen & Haastrup 2004 15–16. The authors observe in an endnote that advocacy for retaining pagan temples did not last very long after the death of Gregory in 604.

[218] Thomas 1997 47–8.

[219] Thomas 1997 48.

[220] In more recent writings Hutton gives greater credence to this pagan influence: "The trappings of late antique and medieval Christianities were taken over wholesale from paganism: the form of sacred buildings themselves and the use of clerical costume, altars, incense, music, veils and cloths, decorative foliage and several seasonal festivals." (Hutton 2009a 217)

between these faces and a pagan deity "was destroyed with the collapse of the Murray thesis" and "could hardly have been argued at all by anybody with a real knowledge of the Middle Ages"; rather it was a late development of Christian origin.[221] In *Triumph* he tones this down, saying its connection with paganism "remains dubious".[222] According to Gary Varner, his argument is misleading. It is true that the artisans who carved these were paid by the Church, but the motif was also found in Classical Rome, whence it was carried throughout Europe by the Roman Army and later, by Christians along pilgrim routes. The church officials who footed the bill for these carvings may not have approved of them or even known what they represented: St. Bernard of Clairvaux complained to the Abbot of St. Thierry in 1125, "What mean those ridiculous [carved] monstrosities in the court of cloisters?" While the foliate head is found in Christian artwork, it preserved its form and probably its meaning from pre-Christian times, among people who were barely Christianised.[223] The Green Man may have emerged in Europe as a representation of Silvanus, the oak-wreathed Roman god of the woods, as evidenced by an early thirteenth century foliate head near Paris inscribed "Silvan".[224]

---

[221] Hutton 1991 316.

[222] Hutton 1999a 435.

[223] Varner 2006 147–9.

[224] Varner 2006 153–4. This carving appears in a series of deities' heads, each with their name inscribed (Varner 2008 58–9). As a pagan god Silvanus was hugely popular, though he now receives disproportionately little attention since so few cult artefacts have survived, his temples having been groves and his idols made of wood. Under the *interpretatio Romana* Silvanus was identified with a number of gods throughout the Roman Empire: the pelt-clad 'Mallet God' or Sucellus in Gaul, Germania and Belgica, horned deities such as Cernunnos and Cocidius in Britain, and Pan in Dalmatia (Silvanus and Pan were also sometimes associated or identified with each other in Latin literature) (Ross 1967 160–162, 165; Dorcey 1992 56–63, 68–70). In Gaul he was closely associated with the Silvanae, triple female divinities, and sometimes with the triple Matronae (Dorcey 45). His cult survived longer than many others — until the late fourth or early fifth century, and possibly much later — since it lacked the public structures most easily suppressed by the Church (temples, priesthood and festivals). Mentions of his worship up to the seventh century may or may not refer to contemporary cult practice, but he remained a character of (fearful) superstition until the thirteenth century (Dorcey 145–6, 186). Ultimately, the nature and extent of the god's link with the foliate mask remain uncertain. Perhaps coincidentally, in Elizabethan pageants we encounter Silvanus again as a 'wild-man' clothed in green and adorned with leaves (Strickland & Strickland 1864 vol. 3, p. 318–9; Mardock 2008 39–40).

Samantha Riches looks in another direction, and links the foliate head, 'Green George' with the proto-Islamic Al-Khidr (identified with St. George), a divinity who personifies the return of spring and is said to have died and been resurrected many times. Having bathed thrice in the Fountain of Youth, his skin and clothes have turned green and he leaves green footprints wherever he walks. He is known as 'Living One' or 'the Green One' (Riches 2000 33; thanks to Wade MacMorrighan for this detail).

Pagan remnants, pagan religions

Hutton has claimed in *Triumph* that few folk traditions are of pagan origin, most being "of doubtful ancient provenance" or invented in the Middle Ages or later.[225] To understand his position on this we must again turn to *Pagan Religions*, where in a brief number of pages he dismisses any possibility of European paganism having survived into the Modern age.

His argument is largely one of semantics: is a given survival actually 'paganism', or is it instead 'magic' or 'superstition' or just 'folk tradition'? — or perhaps a mere 'triviality', as he terms the continuing veneration of springs, wells and trees into the late Middle Ages.[226] His argument is illustrated with lots of things that sound like paganism, but he claims these practices no longer involved the worship of the old gods: they had become cultural customs rather than acts of religious faith. Even where the old gods were explicitly mentioned, as in the *Æcerbot* ritual addressed to "Mother Earth" or oaths sworn by the names of pagan deities, he claims these names had become meaningless doggerel.[227] None of these assertions are actually supported by

---

[225] Hutton 1999a 122.

[226] Hutton 1991 300.

[227] Hutton 1991 294, 298. This doesn't ring true to me, since acts of magic, and particularly oaths, usually reference things of perceived power or importance: swearing by the Tooth Fairy doesn't carry quite the same weight as swearing by God, one's mother or one's immortal soul.

Historian Ramsey MacMullen comments on the obscuring effect of too rigidly defining 'religion' as separate from 'culture' . . . 'the way of doing things':

> To the extent that Christianity today remains centered in a book, while it is also the lens through which "religion" may be and most often is defined, the understanding of this term will screen out much that an anthropologist or historian would rather include: it will screen out, it will simply not allow as "religion", dancing and other communal or individual cult acts.

He cites examples of a number of authors who (like Hutton) "[put] into separate boxes, on the one hand, 'practices,' 'festivities,' 'custom,' or 'rituals,' and on the other hand 'worshipped.' The possibility that they all belong in one and the same box doesn't occur." (MacMullen 1997 106) This may be especially so in the case of paganism: Meg Twycross and Sarah Carpenter point out that the word *pagani* when accurately translated referred more to local superstition and festivity than to any official state religion (Twycross &

his sparse endnotes, yet from Hutton's perspective, these people had signalled their conversion to Christianity by the adoption of Christian worship and customs, and he maintains that in so doing, they necessarily abandoned the old gods: one cannot be both Christian and pagan. This assumption of mutual exclusivity is a very important one, as it underpins many of his arguments and effectively circumvents whole areas of inquiry. It is also a simplistic idea locked in a monotheistic mindset: from a more polytheistic and syncretic paradigm such as that of our European ancestors it was quite feasible to accommodate the new Christian God into an existing pantheon without invalidating the older deities.[228]

One particularly rich source for remnants of pagan religion is in the field of folk magic. But this, to Hutton, is an impossibility, since "All the literary sources for European paganism . . . make plain that magic of any kind was not connected with the worship of deities".[229] This bizarre notion is disproven in numerous texts from Greek antiquity,[230] and in the Norse and Icelandic texts as well, though Hutton contends these are not reflective of paganism.[231] Even if we didn't have these examples, literary sources are non-existent (or virtually non-existent) for large areas of the pagan world, and such scanty scraps as we do have could in no way "make plain" that magic was never connected with deity worship throughout the whole of Europe!

To demonstrate that magic need not be connected with paganism, Hutton points to the Florentine Platonists, who he says "gave a respectable philosophical and the-

---

Carpenter 2002 27).

[228] Augustine had to remind his congregation, "God doesn't wish to be worshipped along with those other [pagan deities], not even if he is worshipped a great deal more and those others a great deal less". The worship of other gods alongside the Christian one was a major problem for the early Church. (Mac-Mullen 1997 144–146)

[229] Hutton 1991 291. This distinction is vital to Hutton's thesis, since as he himself affirms, forms of ancient folk magic have survived intact in most parts of Europe to within living memory (p. 292).

[230] For example, in the Greek magical papyri (Betz 1992), or in theurgic practice, as Don Frew has pointed out (1998); Greek writers like Pausanias and Herodotus describe many miraculous goings-on connected with regional cults; in Hellenistic Egypt the gods (Isis, Osiris, Horus, Anubis, Typhon) dispensed magical powers (Luck 1985 47); and we know that magic was from early times associated with the Greek mystery cults of various deities and with the wandering *telestai* and *mystagogai* (initiators) (Dickie 2003 41, 43).

[231] The heathen gods are closely associated with magic throughout these texts, particularly Odin and Freyja (from whom the two principal types of magic, *galdur* and *seidh*, respectively originate). Most texts date from the early Christian period and probably contain a degree of Christian colouring, but not all. The Norse *Hávamál* and *Sigrdrífumál* are dated by most historians to the heathen period (Page 2006 110): in the former, the gods create the magic runes and Odin gifts them to mankind; in the latter, a Valkyrie gives instructions on runic charms, including some which are to be accompanied by prayers to deities such as Tyr and the Norns.

The German Merseburg incantations, recorded in the ninth or tenth century, are the only surviving magic charms in Old High German that don't show an obvious influence from Christianity. These clearly connect Odin, Freyja, Fulla and other deities with magic. (Jeep 2001 112–3) Odin or Wodan is also connected with magic in the tenth century Old English *Nine Herbs Charm*.

ological basis to the study and employment of spiritual powers by devout Christians".[232] Actually, this group were about as pagan as you could get without being killed for it, and were under constant suspicion of heresy. The man who inspired the founding of their Platonic Academy, Gemistos Plethon, privately advocated a return to a polytheistic religion of Hellenistic gods,[233] and its leading light, Marsilio Ficino, promoted a merging of Christianity with the philosophies and ecstatic polytheistic rites of ancient Orphism. For Ficino, the archetypal powers of the universe were personified in the Greek deities, and the invocations he sang to these gods on his lyre seem to have been his highest form of spiritual expression.[234] This school, at the very heart of the Italian Renaissance, is in fact a fine example of the kind of syncretism between Christianity and pagan polytheism that Hutton has deemed impossible.

It is perhaps worth a digression to look more closely at the Platonic Academy's founding inspiration, Gemistos Plethon (born between 1355 and 1360, died 1452). He had a huge influence on the Italian Renaissance, and was also one of the leaders of a Byzantine revival which, but for the Turkish invasion, might have resulted in a separate Greek-speaking Renaissance centred on Constantinople.[235] Hutton's sketch of this man in a more recent essay, *Paganism in the Lost Centuries* (in *Witches, Druids and King Arthur*),[236] hardly conveys his remarkable pagan leanings, nor the suspicion with which he was viewed by orthodoxy. Hutton is unnecessarily pessimistic of our ability to understand Plethon's beliefs, given that many of his writings survive; Hutton claims, for instance, that his *Book of Laws* or *Nomoi* is entirely lost to us except through fragments quoted by his enemies. In fact, whole chapters of the radically pagan tract survive;[237] its key points are also summarised in Plethon's brief *Summary of the Doctrines of Zoroaster and Plato*, which begins by bluntly stating "The gods really exist", names Zeus as their chief, and encourages us to "be prudent" in acknowledging them.[238] Compare with Hutton's statement that "In none of [Plethon's extant writings] did he recommend paganism as such".

Hutton is also aware of only a single student, Kabakes, who was entrusted with Plethon's secret beliefs, despite the fact that a number of followers continued to de-

---

[232] Hutton 1991 292.

[233] Webb 1989 214.

[234] Voss 2002. The *Orphic Hymns* were also used by a number of Ficino's acquaintances, such as Pico della Mirandola, who says: "Nothing is more effective in natural magic than the hymns of Orpheus, if the right kind of music, intention of the mind, and other circumstances are applied which are only known to the wise". Compare with Hutton's more recent statement that no Renaissance Italians ever "got sufficiently carried away . . . to have revived rites to pagan deities" (2003a 177).

[235] Godwin 2005 10.

[236] Hutton 2003a 173–6.

[237] They can be read in summary in Woodhouse 2000, 322–356.

[238] Woodhouse 2000 319–320.

fend his pagan writings after his death;[239] Marsilio Ficino was said to have inherited from him "an ancient tradition of pagan theology that led directly from Zoroaster, Hermes Trismegistus, Orpheus, and Pythagoras to Plato and his followers".[240] Indeed, rumours of the Book of Laws and its contents were circulating ten, possibly twenty years before Plethon's death, and sections of it seem to have been separately published and distributed; the *Summary* may have been intended for Plethon's initiates.[241] Plethon was lucky enough to end his life in confinement in Mistra; one of his admirers, Iouvenalios, was executed for apostasy by having his ears and tongue cut out and his limbs broken, then being taken out to sea and thrown overboard alive.[242]

Plethon studied at Adrianopolis or Brusa with the learned Jew Eliseus, who seems to have been a Zoroastrian and a polytheist, and who introduced Plethon to Averroes, Proclus and Zoroaster.[243] It is tempting, then, to wonder whether this Eliseus ever met with the philosophies of the Sabians of Harran (further south-east in Anatolia), who had long resisted conversion to either Christianity or Islam, and openly retained their polytheistic paganism into the eleventh century; beyond this time they became more hidden and merged with esoteric Muslim sects, various of which were still accused of perpetuating these pagan philosophies into the fourteenth century.[244] The Sabians' beliefs certainly fit well with Plethon's, compassing Greek hermeticism, astrology and alchemy, and a pantheon of Classical gods identified with the planets and the heavens. Harran even housed a Platonic Academy, and had once been a haven for the greatest pagan thinkers of Europe, fleeing Christian persecution.[245]

---

[239] Woodhouse 2000 363–4.

[240] Woodhouse 2000 373.

[241] Woodhouse 2000 318–9.

[242] Woodhouse 35, 272, 315–7; DeBolt 1998.

[243] Woodhouse 23–27; Gottheil 1906; Idel 2002 143–5.

[244] Green 1992 133; MacMullen 1997 29. Pierre Chuvin has also sought a link between Harran and Plethon (1990 149–50).

[245] Green 1992 167. In the late stages of writing this article I finally managed to read Don Frew's article *Harran: Last Refuge of Classical Paganism* (Frew 1999), which provides fascinating information on the city and on channels through which it influenced European philosophy (though it says nothing of Plethon or Eliseus). Frew reminds us that the *Picatrix*, considered the basis of the European grimoire tradition, and the *Hermetica*, the most important document of Renaissance magic, both derived from Harranian paganism. This would contradict Hutton's position that scholarly mediæval forms of magic "were distinctively the products of the Christendom at the time" (Hutton 1991 292). Frew also states: "I now believe that a direct line of transmission can be traced from the hermetic and Neoplatonic theurgy of late antiquity to the beginnings of the modern Craft movement". I eagerly await the book I understand Frew is preparing, which is to more fully explain all the links in this transmission.

Hutton has also read Frew's article, and seemingly in response devoted a large section of his essay *Paganism in the Lost Centuries* to Harran and the influence it might or might not have had on European magic (2003a 137–174). He is at pains to emphasise any inconsistencies or uncertainties regarding our sources for Harranian philosophy. Specialists in the history of Harran such as Tamara Green are much less hesitant than Hutton in naming the key features of Harranian religion, and they chart a far longer period of religious development than he does (Green claims three thousand years with no radi-

Let's return to *Pagan Religions* and the Italian Renaissance. Of other Renaissance figures, Hutton names Botticelli and Michelangelo as two devoutly Christian artists who depicted pagan gods for aesthetic rather than devotional purposes.[246] He seems unaware that Botticelli, and almost certainly Michelangelo as well, were Neoplatonic mystics, with a deep reverence for Hellenic polytheism.[247] But he uses this example to prepare us for a much more momentous idea: that most of what we *think* we know about Irish, Norse and Germanic mythology is wrong, because most of our sources are — like the works of Botticelli and Michelangelo — non-devotional, romanticised depictions. Furthermore, he tells us, these depictions are not even retellings of native myth, but are, on the whole, rehashings of themes from Christian and Classical mythology, translated into a 'local' style. Thus the Norns are "generally accepted among scholars" to be the Greek Fates transferred to a Teutonic setting, "and had no native equivalents".[248] In fact, most scholars connect the Norns with the

---

cal disruptions; Hutton, two hundred). Hutton, however, characterises all other scholars specialising in Harran as having "explained away" contradictions to make their reconstructions "seem more plausible", and suggests as an alternative "that the surviving sources are so defective, on so many grounds, that there is actually no real primary material, and therefore that nothing absolutely certain can be said about the subject" (Hutton 2003a 149).

Hutton's essay continues with a brief summary of Neoplatonism, hermeticism and natural magic in Europe, and key figures in its transmission (including Plethon). It silently corrects several inaccuracies from Hutton's previous books, for instance regarding Botticelli's pagan interests (see below) or Pan's status among Neoplatonists. At the same time it advances a number of unlikely new claims, such as that Plato was the first of the ancients to declare planets and stars to be divine (p. 157; Greek and other mythologies fill the heavens with stellar gods and demi-gods; see for example Hesiod's *Theogony*, *Works and Days*, and surviving fragments of the Hesiodic *Astronomia*, which gives the stories of the constellations), or that the pagan survivals postulated by Ludo Milis and his collaborators (Milis 1998) are flatly impossible (Hutton having neither engaged with any of their arguments nor even touched on their subject matter; p. 192). I shall not attempt a full critique of *Paganism in the Lost Centuries* here.

[246] Hutton 1991 295.

[247] Botticelli was the first to make Greek myth the subject of a large canvas, and his purpose was to reproduce a famous artwork of the ancient world described by Lucian; his later work, "Birth of Venus", was intended to express Neoplatonic ideals (Griffiths 1988 114–5). Frances Yates believes Botticelli's *Primavera* was magically constructed to transmit the powers of the favourable planetary deities, in much the same way that a theurgist would magically cause a statue to be inhabited by the god it represented (Yates 1964 77).

Michelangelo was from his youth surrounded by influential Neoplatonists and seems very likely to have been one himself (Balas 1995 25–9). A letter to him from fellow Neoplatonist Sebastiano del Piombo may indicate his approach to Christian themes in his artwork: Sebastiano recommends that he depict the rape of Ganymede on the Medici Chapel cupola, suggesting that the addition of a halo would allow it to be mistaken for St. John of the Apocalypse being carried to heaven (Balas 30). This has been interpreted by some as a joke, but it may have an element of truth: Michelangelo's contemporary Pietro Aretino certainly believed he disguised pagan imagery in his work, and that his supposed Christian piety was a sham (Balas 32–3). Michelangelo's statue "Bacchus" (mentioned by Hutton) is of course the central deity of Orphism.

[248] Hutton 1991 296. Similarly, "It is very likely that when writing of the Tuatha de Danaan [sic], the Irish were not recording something in which their ancestors actually believed but fitting old deities into

Matres and Matrones — triads of female deities venerated in north-western Europe until at least the fifth century — and other native divinities.[249] He similarly proposes that Odin's self-sacrifice for the runes is a thinly-veiled imitation of the crucifixion of Christ, and while he allows that "present-day scholars are divided over whether it is a Christian poem or not", for him it is all "surely too much to be coincidental".[250] In fact, present-day scholars are largely united in considering Odin's hanging from the tree to be an ancient theme tied to shamanistic journeying and initiation. If anything, when Christian and pagan iconography are mingled, as in the tenth-century Jelling stone, the unfamiliar newcomer Jesus seems to adopt imagery from Odin, rather than the other way round.[251] It is generally accepted that some colouring from Christianity has occurred in the Norse myths, but Hutton's suggestion that such myths therefore tell us little about the earlier religion is extreme and unsupported. He attempts to distance the surviving Welsh myths from earlier paganism in the same way, relying on a misreading of previous scholarship.[252] Hutton's insistence that any case for

a structure inspired by the Greek pantheon" (Hutton 1991 296). It is worth noting that, while some tales of the Tuatha Dé Danann are certainly hybridised with Christian and Latin themes (notably those in the genre of *immrama* or 'voyage tales'), in other cases there is confirming evidence of their pagan origin. For instance, the stories of the hero Lug are very similar to the independently-surviving Welsh tales of Lleu and Llefelys, pointing to a common origin in the myths of the Celtiberian god Lugus (Koch 2006 994).

[249] Hutton seems to have misconstrued Rudolf Simek, who notes the possibility that the Norns' grouping as a triad could be a Classical borrowing, but affirms that a "plurality of women of fate" has its basis in Germanic paganism (Simek 1996 236–7; see also p. 79). The Norns as a triad certainly predate the Christian Snorri Sturlusson, appearing in the *Völuspá*. As individuals or groups of unspecified number they are also common in skaldic poetry from the tenth century or earlier: Hallfred Óttarson vandrædaskáld, for example, spoke of his conversion from paganism and the "long-maintained fates of the norns" he had thus escaped. A similar sentiment is found in graffiti carved in the twelfth-century Borgund stave church at Sogn, Norway: "Thórir carved these runes on St. Olaf's day when he came by here. The norns did both good and bad. They shaped a lot of sorrow for me." Unlike the Greek Fates, the Norns were never limited to three in number, even in later texts: the principal Norns were a triad, but there were other classes of Norn, including a great number who measured out the fates of individual people (Lindow 2002 245). As well as the Matres and Matrones, the Norns have probable connection to the threefold goddess whose cult Saxo Grammaticus describes in Denmark around 1200, the Wyrds attested to by Chaucer, and the Weird Sisters described in Holinshed's sixteenth century *Chronicles*, from which Shakespeare drew the plot of *Macbeth* (Jones & Pennick 1997 150).

[250] Hutton 1991 297.

[251] Kure 2006 68–71. Odin has early connection with hanging and the hanged. In skaldic poetry Odin was "lord of the gallows" and "god of the hanged", as well as being himself "the hanged" and "load of the gallows" (Patton 2009 224). The eighth century Lärbro Stora Hammars stone in Gotland depicts a man being hanged from a tree as a probable sacrifice to Odin (Patton 225, 227). See also Davidson 1965 51–2, 143–5; Lindow 2002 321–2. In equating Odin with Jesus, Hutton is essentially repeating the argument of Sophus Bugge, who in the late nineteenth century conceded defeat to Victor Rydburg's masterly demonstration of the myth's pagan origins (Dronke 1992; thanks to Carla O'Harris for this detail).

[252] For instance, he proposes that the Welsh Cerridwen was originally a simple sorceress character invented for the *Hanes Taliesin* (*Tale of Taliesin*), only later to be reinvented as a goddess in poems such

a pre-Christian survival must "prove" itself with "firm evidence" is at odds with the many unsupported (and unsupportable) assertions he himself has liberally scattered throughout *Pagan Religions.*

The rest of Hutton's Middle Ages are peppered with examples of 'folklore' and its repression by the Church, or as he prefers to call it, "a series of initiatives by unusually stringent prelates against practices which the local people, and indeed, most churchmen, would probably have considered to be Christian."[253] A recent work by Emma Wilby summarises rather well these "Christian" practices in the British Isles at the end of the Middle Ages. Pagan gods and nature spirits were thinly disguised as countless saints who were worshipped throughout the British countryside. The most important Christian festivals, such as Christmas and Easter, were still obviously built around pre-Christian customs, which were even more blatantly apparent in secular celebrations such as fairs and harvest festivals. There was widespread ignorance of the Christian faith, since a significant proportion of the population did not attend church, and in many areas of Scotland and England the parishes did not even have a priest. Even among regular church-goers many showed little interest or comprehension, and priests complained that their congregations could not repeat rudimentary Christian doctrine, and knew more about Robin Hood than Jesus Christ.[254] Despite

---

as *The Chair of Cerridwen* by the Gogynfeirdd poets of the eleventh to fourteenth centuries. According to Hutton these poets produced some of the most visionary tales, but they "created a new mythology, instead of merely working with characters from pagan legend. They did this by elevating human or semi-human characters to the status of deities." (1991 322–3) This is terribly confused. The *Hanes Taliesin* is not early but very *late* in the literary tradition, dating from the sixteenth century. Hutton cites the Welsh scholar Sir Ifor Williams for his claim that the composition's language dates it to the ninth century, but Williams says nothing of the sort! Rather, he says that certain *themes and fragments* of the work are old: in particular, it shows the influence of earlier Taliesin poems such as *The Chair of Cerridwen*. Hutton has the chronology reversed! Williams also postulates that both early and late works surrounding this shape-changing bard-magician Taliesin reflect a popular Taliesin myth which appeared some time after 900, but which incorporates elements of older pagan Celtic mythology and folklore. Hutton's entire argument about Cerridwen not having been a goddess thus evaporates. (Williams 1944 ch. 3. Hutton cites ch. 4, but there only are three chapters.)

[253] Hutton 1991 299.

[254] Priests themselves were not always aloof from popular custom. Hutton cites the example of the priest at Inverkeithing in Fife who in 1282 gathered the young girls of the town and led them in a dance around the churchyard carrying a large carved wooden phallus on a pole, singing licentious songs and performing lewd actions. Some of his congregation, Hutton tells us, were "forced" to strip and whip each other (although according to Jeffery Russell this occurred on a separate occasion, when the priest prescribed the whipping as a penance to some penitents [Russell 1972 164]). Hutton claims that the priest, being mentally disturbed, was then killed by a parent of one of the girls, and that his actions couldn't be considered representative of any more widespread custom (1991 299). What he doesn't tell us is that the priest's murder (in what was described as an unseemly brawl) took place a year after the churchyard dance, and that in the meantime he had been accused before his bishop by some of the more modest of his congregation, but had successfully defended himself on the grounds that this rite was in common usage in the country. He was allowed to retain his benefice (Wright 1865 32). This was far from an isolated instance.

this, these people's spiritual lives were far from empty, for they held complex beliefs around magic, the dead, fairies and the otherworld, and regularly employed magic charms themselves or turned to cunning men and women for help with more serious problems.[255]

Other scholars have argued that the sixteenth and seventeenth century European witch hunts "were provoked by the Church striving to enforce orthodoxy on areas which were officially Christian, but in fact were still dominated by pre-Christian magic beliefs. Witch-hunting meant the often forcible subjection of remote, outlying regions to Christianity, where previously the Church's power had been recognized only formally."[256]

Hutton is not entirely oblivious to the otherworldly beliefs of these people, and actually mentions some of them briefly, as a tantalising historical unknown, a "vivid medieval realm of the imagination which extended across the whole of Europe and through most of the period" and which "urgently requires further investigation". Clearly he is still, when writing *Pagan Religions*, unaware of the work of Ginzburg, Henningsen and other witchcraft historians who have provided the "Sustained and thorough research" he says is so sorely needed. Had he read their works at this point his entire section on pagan survivals might have been very different.

We have numerous accounts of amorous and sexual dances held in churches and churchyards in Britain and Europe throughout the Middle Ages (the celebrants "behaving just like pagans"), and William Tydeman suggests that the same tendencies amongst the clergy may have prompted the church to grudgingly support the Feast of Fools as a safe channel for these impulses. (Tydeman 1979 15–16)

[255] Wilby 2005 12–21. Robin Briggs paints a similar picture of Early Modern France, where the church struggled (and failed) to effectively Christianise a populace that still retained an animistic world-view; they were viewed as pagans by church authorities (Briggs 1995). Hutton himself has illustrated how stubbornly people can hold on to old religious beliefs. In *Stations of the Sun* he describes official attempts to eradicate Christmas in Scotland (and elsewhere in Britain) during the Reformation. Despite hawkish observation by the Kirk and the threat of harsh penalties including excommunication, there was initially open opposition, which gave way to secret religious services and even community-wide celebrations that in truth were concealed only from the kirkmen. In remote areas Christmas celebrations continued largely unaltered, with only the official service missing, and some areas of the Outer Hebrides "effectively never experienced a Reformation at all" (Hutton 1996 ch. 3; p. 32). Even though the Scottish ban on Christmas lasted only a century, it provides an intriguing comparison to the more long-standing repression of pagan worship, and makes me wonder why Hutton remains so immune to the idea of pagan survivals.

[256] Kahk 1989 276. Kahk cites Hugh Trevor-Roper as one of these scholars, and himself illustrates the jeering disdain Estonian peasants had for the Christian faith and clergy; they continued to meet openly for sacrifice at sacred sites until the end of the seventeenth century (p. 283).

Revel and ritual

Many folk customs still surviving today are popularly believed to be pagan in origin. Hutton is convinced otherwise, and states that the majority of these "are either of doubtful ancient providence or (more often) developed in the Middle Ages or later". He points us for evidence to his previous book, *Stations of the Sun*.[257] One such custom centres on the figure of Father Christmas, who he claims was a literary invention of seventeenth-century England, subsequently conflated with the Santa Claus of the New York Dutch — this American Santa Claus being himself largely born out of the imagination of Clement Clark Moore in 1822.[258] This is served up with Hutton's customary wit, but what he doesn't tell us is that Santa Claus and Father Christmas both derive from characters in remarkably similar Christmas-time masquerades: mummers plays in Britain and belsnickling plays (from *Peltz-Nichol*, 'fur-Nichol') among the New York Dutch. Both characters originated, by slightly different routes, in the same 'wild-man' performances of Europe, and although both underwent a number of metamorphoses over the centuries, they retained their most identifiable wild-man attributes, including their rowdy nature, cross-dressing, black faces and animal disguises. (It may seem a strange twist of fate that the two should recombine after so many years, but perhaps the similarity of their rôles helped them to gravitate together.) Phyllis Siefker has chronicled in detail the development of both Santa Claus and Father Christmas from common origins in mediæval and earlier masquerades.[259] Santa Claus, though he now takes the name of St. Nicholas,

---

[257] Hutton 1999a 122.

[258] Hutton 1999a 8; 1996 117–9.

[259] Siefker 1996. 'Mumming' as a house-visiting custom is well documented from the Middle Ages, however its format has changed over the years. It seems to have adopted its modern textual format from popular theatre traditions, such as Harlequinades, Robin Hood plays and English broadsides, from the seventeenth century on. (Millington 2002 56, 97, 139–140, 154–157). Of course, Harlequin himself is yet another variant of the same wild-man figure (Siefker 107–122).

  To my mind the most promising suggestion for the origin of mumming, despite Hutton's protestations (Hutton 1996 77–8), is that of Gareth Morgan, who links it with the *momoeri* of Northern Turkey and similar traditions in Greece, and proposes that the ritual drama first came to Flanders with Flemish cru-

was earlier a much more fearsome figure called "Black Pete", the saint's side-kick in a good-cop-bad-cop routine. On the English side, the wild-man character bifurcated and multiplied, and now appears in the guise of Father Christmas, Old Tosspot and Beelzebub, the last of which probably resembles Peltz-Nichol the most.[260] Hutton disdains early theories linking Father Christmas and Santa Claus with shamanism or pagan deities,[261] apparently oblivious to the strength such theories gain in light of the work of Ginzburg and others. Siefker's study of the various European cavalcade performances is along rather different lines to Ginzburg's, but she independently arrives at some very similar conclusions, connecting them with a rich magical folklore spread across Europe and Asia, which has its ultimate origins in an ancient central-Eurasian proto-shamanism.[262]

---

saders and their staff who were based in the area. Hutton cites Craig Fees' criticisms of Morgan, but fails to detect the errors in Fees' case. For a start, Fees was substantially misled by an editorial addition to Morgan's article, so that he misunderstood what data Morgan was relying on. Fees also proposed, rather creatively, that because the Greek term *momoeri* is first attested in the twentieth century, it could have been adopted by the Greeks from visiting English scholars who had watched their dramas some years earlier. This suggestion ignores Morgan's analysis of the word, its meaning in Greek ('scurrilous old men') and the prevalence of analogous terms for performers in related traditions throughout Greece, Macedonia, Thrace and the Cyclades (Morgan 1989; Fees 1989). In balance, Morgan's evidence and arguments stack up exceptionally well, while not constituting proof. Intriguingly, one author has suggested that a Thracian variant of the play may have derived from ancient Dionysian rites, since it featured a 'baby' carried in a *liknon* (winnowing fan) by the 'old lady' Babo (described as a nurse, foster-mother or unmarried mother) (Dawkins 1906). This recalls to us the *liknon* in which Dionysus or Iacchus was placed after his birth, in a scene repeated in numerous mystic rites and initiations of the ancient world, including, probably, those at Eleusis. The Eleusinian myth has Iacchus in the care of the obscene old nurse Baubo (Harrison 1903; Marcovich 1988 23). The continuance of Greek Dionysian festivals until the twelfth century is well attested, and descriptions of those festivities are very reminiscent of modern Greek mumming (Lawson 2003 221–6).

If mumming was indeed a thirteenth-century Flemish import from Greece or Asia Minor, wouldn't that rule out the possibility that it preserves relics of Western European or British paganism? Perhaps, and perhaps not. When mumming was taken up by black slaves in early nineteenth-century Trinidad, they invested it with meaning from their own diaspora religion, so that the Beelzebub-like lead character became 'Papa Bois', a forest and vegetation divinity also known as 'Gran Bois' in the Haitian Vodou religion (Siefker 1996 26–30). The presence of ancient wild-man and fairy themes among the various European Mumming variants seem to testify to a similar process of assimilation.

[260] Both Beelzebub and Peltz-Nichol are fearsome and threatening, dress in furs, and carry a whip or club; both throw treats for the children, then whip them as they try to pick them up. Both represent the Devil. Another character, the transvestite 'Betsy', was earlier a representative of the Earth Mother in Mediaeval plough pageants (Berger 2001 80–81). Hutton, in *Pagan Religions*, is in rare agreement regarding Beelzebub and the 'old woman': the former he identifies as "apparently, that deity known in Ireland as the Daghda and in Gaul as Sucellus, who was always carrying this weapon and a vessel"; and the latter, "[p]erhaps 'she' was once a patronal goddess". He does not link Beelzebub with Father Christmas. (Hutton 1991 328–9)

[261] Hutton 1999a 128; 1996 119.

[262] Siefker's is not an academic work, and it contains some conjectures that are bound to be controversial, but it also gathers an excellent array of information on wild-man and black-face traditions in a single

70

Other traditions are discounted by Hutton in a similar manner because rather than remaining static over the centuries they have metamorphosed or hybridised in modern times — though one might argue that innovations are a hallmark of living traditions. Does the fact that the Padstow Obby Oss (for example) was amalgamated from other traditions in the late 1700s make it any less 'pagan'?[263] The answer to such

---

volume.

[263] Hutton 1999b 30. In *Pagan Religions* Hutton's conclusions were very different: he declared that modern animal mask and hobby-horse traditions originated in pagan revels, such as the Kalends of January, which were censured by St. Aldhelm in the seventh century and Theodore Archbishop of Canterbury around 700. Hutton tells us that Aldhelm "expressed horror at the wearing of animal costumes (especially of stags) by revellers", while Theodore raged at revellers who wore animal skins and heads to transform themselves into beasts, or cross-dressed as old women. "All these complaints were unavailing. Animal masks continued to take many ritual forms up till the modern period" including hobby-horse entertainments, midwinter horse-skull traditions and the Abbots Bromley horn dance (1991 329).

By the time he wrote *Stations* he had realised that the passage attributed to Theodore was in fact a later interpolation by a French or German copyist, and he pointed out the error of those scholars who had believed the attribution (without mentioning that he himself was amongst them). More mysteriously, he changed his tune on Aldhelm as well, and says nothing of animal costumes or revelry, instead briefly stating that St. Aldhelm had spoken of the former worship of *ermula* ('pillars/statues') of the snake and the stag in pagan shrines and that "the passage has absolutely no connection with seasonal rites, at midwinter or any other time." (1996 89–90) He gives no explanation for his earlier, contradictory account. In a remarkable reversal from *Pagan Religions*, he then states that midwinter animal disguises in the early Middle Ages are attested only on the Continent, and that there is is a yawning gap (and "no demonstrable links") between these and the first waist-mounted hobby-horses appearing in England (in the late Middle Ages), let alone animal-head customs, which only appeared in the nineteenth century (1996 93).

The divide he thus creates between Britain and Europe ignores the permeable relationship between these cultures, and risks artificially isolating the British customs of horse-play and animal masquerade. It is just as risky to ignore the broader traditions of masking and guising in Britain, which were popular over long periods. In 1250 Oxford University forbade its students from conducting masked revels with dancing and fights about the church and in the streets. In 1334, 1393 and 1405 the City of London forbade the practice of going through the streets masked and entering houses (as a form of begging). Fourteenth-century Christmas pageants put on for English royalty, and seemingly inspired by folk custom, included celebrants in animal costumes. (Chambers 1996 vol. 1 pp. 92, 141–2, 392–3, 400). The clergy of Wells Cathedral, Somerset were forbidden in the 1330s to perform their theatrical entertainments "bringing in monstrosities [in the form] of terrifying apparitions". A 1418 proclamation forbade mumming at Christmas "with eny feynyd berdes, peyntid visers, disfourmyd faces or colourid visages in eny wyse" (Twycross & Carpenter 2002 42, 85). Later, Shakespeare supplies us with the clownish Forester's Song from *As You Like It* (of which the traditional Cornish May-song *Hal An Tow* is a variant):

> What shall he have that killed the deer? / His leather skin, and horns to wear. / . . .
> Take thou no scorn, to wear the horn; / It was a crest ere thou wast born; / Thy father's
> father wore it, / And thy father bore it. . . (4.2.4)

Is this merely a reference to cuckolds (who by idiom 'wear horns'), or does it also depict a folk custom, well known to the audience of the time? The latter would be much funnier, and would better explain an otherwise bewildering scene. A similarly-clad figure called 'Horne' (Herne the Hunter) appears in *The Merry Wives of Windsor*, although some believe this to be a "mischievous creation" of Shakespeare's (Twycross & Carpenter 2002 31). Later, in 1735–6 we have first mention of 'hooding', the custom associated with the Hooden Horse (which Hutton only traces back to 1807): Samuel Pegge, vicar of Godmersham, de-

questions depends on how one defines 'paganism', and whether such reinventions, if they occur within a Christian society, can legitimately be seen as expressions of non-Christian spirituality. With this question in the back of our minds, let us survey some other folk traditions.

As a morris dancer and mummer I have been struck by the similarity of these two performance traditions to other Whitsunday and Christmas-season festivities on the Continent. The *Căluş* of Romania is one obvious parallel; another is the Christmas revels associated with Frau Holda or Frau Perchta, from the alpine regions of Germany, Austria and northern Switzerland. Here we see the same ritualised begging with blackened faces, costumed dancing, cross-dressing, and general atmosphere of public mayhem.[264] But here the performers are imitating Holda or Perchta — a divinity popularly regarded as queen of the witches for at least the last thousand years — and her subjects, the *perchten*, imps, fairies, witches and hordes of the dead. The twelve days of Christmas were originally the *Zwölften*, an intercalary period consecrated to the dead,[265] and these tumultuous processions from village to village re-enact the Wild Hunt that traditionally rode forth at this time, an ecstatic battling of spectres amongst the clouds which provided the pattern for the stereotyped flight of witches to their sabbath.[266] Similar dances are found throughout Europe, and often have a folkloric association with fairies or spirits, particularly those fairies residing (like Holda or Perchta) in springs and streams. In several traditions the names given to the dancers are similar or identical to the names of the spirits: Slavic *rusalka* is both

scribes it as "a country masquerade at Christmas time, which in Derbyshire they call guising . . . and in other places mumming" (Pegge 1874 82).

Other seemingly relevant details appear in *Stations* but have not been connected by Hutton: the Kalendae ("or rather ancient European festivals of midwinter and New Year which churchmen compared to the Roman Kalendae") were condemned in early eleventh century York as "the nonsense which is performed on New Year's Day in various kinds of sorcery" and in late twelfth century Exeter as "heathen rites" (1996 7). By the thirteenth century the festivities had been taken up by clergy and choirboys in the Feast of Fools, whose celebrants were accused of "inverting the proper order of worship and pretending to praise demons at the New Year"; by the fourteenth century at least, this involved irreverent masked mimes (Hutton 1996 99).

From all this it seems clear that the festival of January Kalends, popular throughout the entire Roman Empire and persisting in various forms to a late date on the Continent, was no less popular or persistent in England. Again and again we hear of revellers wearing masks and disguises; whether *animal* disguises is mostly not stated, but the British attestations are so remarkably similar to those spread across Europe that we can hardly ignore the wider pattern. Even as near as the Channel Isles we find clear precedents for animal-skin and animal-head disguises going back to the sixteenth century (see below), and in mainland France such precedents go back to the pagan era.

Masks have an ancient etymological link to spirits: the words *masca* and *larva* both refer equally to mask and ghost, and in the late Middle Ages became terms for witches (Klaniczay & Pócs 2005 118).

[264]Motz 1984 153; Siefker 1996 162.

[265]Ginzburg 1990 105.

[266]Ginzburg 1990 296–303.

a nymph and a dance, Bulgarian *rousaliy* are dancers related to the *rousalka* or water nymph, and the *cǎluşari* are linked by interchangeable semantics and a complex web of parallels with the *iele* or fairies.[267] During the Russian festival of *Rusal'naia nedelia* young women would jump over a bonfire and then begin mimicking the *rusalka*, trying to catch and tickle the boys. The *rusalka* fairy is, according to some, a remnant of goddess-worship, and some Ukrainian sources call her *bohynia*, 'goddess'.[268] Morris itself has a likely early connection with fairy-lore.[269] And yet all these performances now occur within a Christian culture. Again we must ask, is this sufficient reason to ignore them in our search for pagan remnants? Even today, in a number of European cultures, performances such as these are at the very epicentre of folk magic, and the performers are revered as healers and magicians.

Similar traditions closer to Britain are not hard to find. In Calvinist-era Guernsey, Jersey and Sark we find our familiar Christmas-tide revelry amongst young women and men, whose all-night spinning and knitting parties would often turn into nocturnal rampages (one of the terms used is '*esbat*') in which they would "run unbridled with an infinity of the most scandalous debauchery, to the dishonour of God, ill fame of the country, to the laying to waste of civil behaviour and Christian honesty", singing "profane and lascivious songs", dancing and running from parish to parish, often wearing hideous costumes such as an "artificially re-skinned mare" or in cross-dress, or with blackened faces. Sometimes they stole horses to ride to a distant assembly, then turned them loose; often the revellers themselves would wear a harness and be ridden (I can't help but recall English witchcraft testimonies quoted by Margaret Murray in which witches or their victims were fitted with a harness and ridden like a beast![270]). There was often an element of begging, recalling the black-faced English guisers or mummers, and like many of their counterpart revellers on the Continent, they broke into people's gardens and houses to steal food or make sexual advances to young women. In the late nineteenth century similar traditions still persisted, complete with hobby-horses much like the Welsh Mari Lwyd or the

---

[267] Kligman 1977 2, 54–5.

[268] Rappoport 1999; see also Ginzburg 1990 190–1.

[269] Morris is widely thought to come from the word 'Moorish', after the dancers' blackened faces, and variants in Spain and Portugal are called 'Morisca'. Strangely enough, in Spain and Portugal 'moor' need not indicate racial type, but can connote general foreignness, paganism or otherworldliness: unbaptised children may be called 'muoro', and spirits dwelling in caves, rocks and springs are said to be *muora encantada*, enchanted Moorish princesses. (Kligman 1977 60–61) Most Portuguese towns have a local legend of such a fairy, and in some cases she is a spinning fairy, '*moura-fiandeira*' (Gallop 1936 pp. 77–81). In Basque folklore, *mairu* (plural *mairuak*) is both 'Moor' and 'fairy' (Barandiarán 2009 88). In Greek folklore, Ἀράπηδες are both Arabs and fairies, as well as being characters in mumming plays (Lawson 2003 211, 224). From the earliest times, a blackened face seems to have signified a ghost; by the sixteenth century it had become a devil (Twycross & Carpenter 2002 11–12).

[270] Murray 1963 236. Transformations of bridled humans into horses are also attested in Hungarian witch-trials (Pócs 1999 79–80).

73

Hoden Horse of Kent; we are told that in Sark's farmhouses "there was always . . . a stock of horse-skulls in hand for the occasion", the population being "wont to disguise themselves in the hides and with the heads of a variety of beasts".[271] In the Calvinist Guernsey records there is also occasional mention of the Guernsey practise of 'were-wolfery' ('*vouarouverie*'). This term seemed to indicate coursing around the country-side by night, "chasing women, eating prodigiously, getting be-smattered with mud, and 'caterwauling' generally", but it also perhaps links the revellers with those European 'werewolves' accused of witchcraft, who claimed that far from being evil, they ran and fought for the fertility of the land. Such 'werewolf' beliefs have been identified by Carlo Ginzburg, Éva Pócs and others as an ancient motif associated with shamanism, death and resurrection, the covering of oneself with animal skins being morphologically linked to both the caul and the funeral shroud. Throughout European folklore skins or veils are used to pass between the realms of life and death, and their wearers were said to experience shape-changing, flying and fighting in ecstasy.[272]

One of the most enigmatic details from the Guernsey records is an account we have from the St. Martin parish register: in the evening of December 26, 1630, a group of youths were returning from town, "uttering hugely scandalous enormities"; one was saying that it was "good weather to go about in werewolfery", while four others of his company "in a huddle under a thorn bush" gave him "their supplication to go about this aforesaid damnable art". What these four were up to under the bush seems to have been well understood by the parish consistory, as was the nature of the "damnable art" (a phrase otherwise found only in trials for witchcraft) but these details were not recorded.[273]

During the period that these nocturnal romps were causing so much fuss, the Channel Isles were witness to another, far more chilling spectacle: witch trials, complete with hideous tortures, mutilations and public executions. Furthermore, the testimonies of accused witches in Guernsey sound remarkably as though they're describing these self-same revels, complete with 'werewolfery' and black-face disguises: we hear of devils, witches and wizards appearing as a variety of animals, but particularly as dogs (dogs who were much larger than normal, stood on their hind legs and had human hands); and witches smothered in black ointment.[274] This parallel is made even more remarkable by the fact that the revels and witch trials directly coincide in time and space.[275] Take, for example, the enigmatic account from St. Martin,

---

[271] Ogier 1998.

[272] Ginzburg 1990 part 3 ch. 2: "Bones and Skin"; Pócs 1999 78–81, 129–30.

[273] Ogier 1998.

[274] Pitts 1886 2, 20–21.

[275] The Guernsey witch trials were in the period 1563–1634 (Pitts 1886 28), and records of night-time revels cited by Ogier date from 1563 to 1677, but mostly concentrated in the 1620s and early 1630s.

above: the year before, two people had been banished for witchcraft and two others tortured, hanged and burnt; the year after, two were executed and ten banished. All these atrocities took place only a mile and a half from St. Martin, at St. Pierre Port. One woman banished for witchcraft in 1629, Anne Blampied, was presumably a relative of Pierre Blampied, who five years earlier was in trouble for having "gadded by night" in the costume of an "artificially re-skinned mare"; whether they were siblings or cousins I cannot say. What I can say is that the bravery of these Guernsey youth in continuing their custom is astonishing.[276]

The Souling plays of Cheshire, England, unite many of the themes we've seen so far. On nights around All Hallows a gang of black-faced and bizarrely costumed characters would visit each farmhouse performing a death and resurrection play and begging for food and ale. Beelzebub (the Devil himself) presided, and there was a cross-dressed 'old lady', but the central character was arguably the 'Wild Horse', a man disguised with sacking and a horse's skull.[277] Originally there was a gang of Soulers in every village, each with their own highly prized horse-skull (often a generations-old heirloom) without which they couldn't perform. When two gangs met they were obliged to fight, and the losers' horse-skull would be smashed. In 1954 Wilfred Isherwood, leader of the Antrobus cast, commented on the tradition that his great-great grandfather, grandfather, father and uncles had bequeathed to him:

> ... [T]here's a lot of people can't understand it, 'cause it's really our religion. We believe in souling; we believe in ghosts, 'cause we're supposed to be ghosts. Sometimes it's not many of us are real attenders at church; because I think our belief is more sentimental, private. And we all turn out on All Hallows Eve, we just come, and go.[278]

---

[276] And I can only guess why some revellers would be tried as witches and others as disturbers of the peace. Some baillifs presided over many witch-trials during their period of office, others presided over few or none: this may indicate differences of personal conviction or leniency in choosing how to interpret offenses. At some of the 'public disturbance' trials we read that older relatives of the accused who were respected members of the community argued on their behalf. One can barely imagine the tension, in a small community like this, between the desire of some to rout witchcraft and the desire of others to protect their children from the pyre.

[277] Kennedy 1980. The horse, though very lively, is pronounced to be 'dead'. In a remarkably similar Romanian *Căluş* performance I have seen footage of, the horse dies and is explicitly resurrected (the hobby-horse, now rare, used to be a common feature of *Căluş*, the very name *căl-uş* meaning 'little horse'; Beza 1928 47, 50). The begging for food from the cellars mirrors the begging or raiding of food and drink by *benandanti* and Valais mountaineers in Italy, *armiers* in the Pyrenees, werewolves in Livonia and Lithuania, Ossetian *pschavi* and *chevsuri*, Hungarian *táltos*, Swiss *Schurtendiebe* (Ginzburg 1990 89, 158, 162, 191, 194) and numerous other groups, all of which symbolically represented or accompanied the wandering dead; their thirst echoes the myth of the unquenchable thirst of the dead (Ginzburg 159).

[278] Kennedy 1980. Compare with Hutton's claim that folk performers took no spiritual interest in their rituals, nor attributed to them any great age. He disparages early folklorists for imposing interpretations

We have now surveyed a number of folk traditions across Britain and Europe, and without going further we can already see a rich pattern emerging of cathartic revels or rituals ('ceremonies', was the word one Antrobus Souler used) spread over wide areas, built on beliefs in fairies and ghosts of the dead. Many such ceremonies brought fertility, health and wealth, and were considered vital to the well-being of the community; often (even simultaneously) they were associated with witchcraft, and in several cases we know the purpose of these rites was explicitly magical. The rites were held at times associated with fairies and the dead: the twelve days of Yule, Whitsunday, the four seasonal Ember Weeks, All Hallows; or, more generally, at night. In some cases the performers functioned as intermediaries between the human and spirit worlds and were bound by strict ritual laws. They took the shapes of animals, some even leaving their bodies to fly through the air; they fought and feasted. They were at times presided over by a goddess or lady, at times by the Devil.

Associated with these revels we can also discern a densely connected series of fairy motifs, such as female water-divinities associated with pregnancy, childbirth and fate, often in threes; figures with black faces; horses; werewolves and other shape-changing animals. Rather than exploring these themes further I point the interested reader to Carlo Ginzburg's excellent book *Ecstasies: Deciphering the Witches' Sabbath*.

Ethnologist João de Pina-Cabral has examined the "problem of pagan survivals" in detail,[279] and concluded that certain beliefs and practices have had an "uncanny capacity for survival" and a continued popular appeal. He cites the example of Portugal, where the church has repeatedly and enthusiastically suppressed local 'errors' and 'superstitions' throughout the centuries, and has, even in modern times, been able to call on the law for enforcement. In the same country, detailed accounts of the local 'errors' and 'superstitions' survive from shortly after the region was officially Christianised, and fourteen centuries later, virtually the same set of beliefs and practices can still be found.[280] Intriguingly, none of the items on Pina-Cabral's list have

---

that contradicted the beliefs of those they collected the folklore from (1999a, 126–9), only to himself dismiss the beliefs of "virtually all the performers of British calendar customs to whom I talked in the 1960s and 1970s . . . that they were enacting rites of pagan origin" (p. 130).

[279] Pina-Cabral 1992.

[280] These beliefs, practices and rituals are catalogued as including magical practices relating to the sun, moon and stars, praying to the moon, and using the heavenly bodies to predict the future; practices dealing with fire and the hearth; practices dealing with water and purification; the 'cult of the dead' and funeral practices; beliefs surrounding stones, waters, trees, mountains and other natural features; beliefs surrounding time and lucky days, hours, etc.; augury by the behaviour of birds or humans; beliefs about right vs. left sides of things; the use of apotropaic amulets, prayers and exorcisms; and sorcery through spell-formulae, herbs, etc.. Beliefs in the magical use of numbers, and in witches, werewolves, enchanted Mooresses and other non-human or quasi-human entities were not seen by the early church as superstitious, but persist as 'superstitions' today. The cult of pagan deities itself, found in the earlier sources, has its modern Portuguese counterpart in the cult of the Devil (following the Christian policy of demonising

survived *within* the rituals of the Church; rather, they have retained so much popular power that the Church has been unable to control them.[281]

Commentators in all eras have characterised such beliefs and practices as anachronisms of a primitive past, redundant to the current time and always on the verge of disappearing altogether. But this constant "impending demise" is a mirage, says Pina-Cabral, and even today these traditions clearly hold value for many people. So are these still the 'same' beliefs and practices as those of ancient Europe? What has been the nature of their continuity in a society that has changed around them? This is a complex question, he tells us, but he believes that two processes in particular are at play: the first, 'fixity', relates to the ability of certain structures — be they ritual, physical or even textual — to retain value for successive generations, even in the midst of major cultural changes. Their continued relevance to quite different people in different ages is made possible by the fact that these rituals are neither simple actions nor statements: "they are not means of communicating but rather of expressing". The second process, 'recurrence', relates to the apparent ability of certain themes and images to recur in different cultures and time periods without any thread of transmission between them. To explain this he cites Rodney Needham's theory that there are a series of extremely simple "capacities, proclivities and constraints that universally make up human nature"; these 'factors' are few in number and are limited to abstract or perceptual attractions, fears and so on, but they can combine to produce more complex synthetic images, 'archetypes' which may be seen as arising spontaneously out of the human condition. Pina-Cabral believes that the processes of 'fixity' and 'recurrence' work together, with the persistent structures of traditional belief and practice ('fixity') providing a context and channel within which archetypal ideas can constantly re-emerge ('recurrence'). Thus, the fixed ritual forms are continuously reinvested with the same recurrent meaning.[282]

A witch would perhaps agree that 'fixity' and 'recurrence' have been key to the survival of our beliefs; they might, however, explain 'recurrence' in slightly different terms, and suggest that the perennial archetypes of the magical realm have some kind of existence in their own right, rather than simply being side-effects of the human psyche. Pina-Cabral might see our Goddess and God, for example, as having constantly re-arisen in the human mind, created and re-created in response to primal needs; a witch, on the other hand, might feel that we are *the Gods'* creations serving

previous deities). Interestingly, throughout the centuries churchmen too have counted among these believers and practitioners, even to the present day. Pina-Cabral believes these findings would not surprise any ethnographer who has done field-work in Europe.

[281] Pina-Cabral notes that literal belief in such 'superstitions' seems unnecessary for them to have power over the human imagination, or to have a strong placebo or nocebo action.

[282] Pina-Cabral also believes that the ascription of 'paganness' to these beliefs and practices is constantly reaffirmed by the sense of their belonging to a distant past, and that their aura of mystery is further enhanced by their failure to conform to the mainstream. From this mysteriousness they gain power.

their purposes, and that their constancy in our dreams and visions is evidence of a greater magical reality.

Ultimately, we have found no simple answer to our repeated question: can certain long-standing traditions be considered 'pagan survivals'? If we define 'paganism' in terms of time and place then the answer is probably 'no', since these traditions no longer exist within the 'pagan period' or within a 'pagan culture'. Some historians have roughly adopted this usage. But if, on the other hand, we seek to understand 'paganism' in terms of its forms and functions, the answer may be 'yes'. Most Neo-pagans, I believe, use the word in this latter sense, optimistic that despite the intervening centuries they still share some common understanding or experience with humans of the past. Pina-Cabral's theory would seem to support their conviction, and it should be clear by now how little there is in Hutton's work — first appearances notwithstanding — to undermine it. Ultimately, it remains entirely reasonable to ask whether paganism has survived to the present day, and whether witchcraft is one expression of that paganism — reasonable, that is, given certain (entirely reasonable) usages of the terms 'paganism' and 'witchcraft'. Hutton's usage differs, and there our ways part.

Other critiques of Hutton's work

In critiquing Professor Hutton's work I am keenly aware of our differing academic qualifications in the field of history — I have none — so I have been encouraged to find I am not alone in my concerns. Hutton's earlier book *Pagan Religions* has been strongly criticised. It has a similarly grand goal to *Triumph*: it seeks to demolish the concept of the ancient Mother- or Earth-Goddess and demonstrate that Neopaganism has no basis in the old religions of Europe. According to Max Dashu it is full of "factual errors, mischaracterizations, and outright whoppers", and she provides counter-examples to several sweeping claims, such as that Breton megaliths "are the only prehistoric monuments in western Europe to bear the unmistakeable figure of a female", that the oldest megaliths in the world are European, or that there is "no trace" of a triple goddess in the Irish and Welsh texts. According to her the book demonstrates strong anti-feminism and an ignorance (or ignoring) of the fields of linguistics and folklore, and misrepresents opposing theories to construct straw-doll arguments.[283] Hutton in response characterised her as not "an academic of any sort" (she studied at Harvard) but "a professional artist whose ideological stance is one of dedicated and extreme feminism", and he declined to address any of the points she raised.[284]

Asphodel Long has also reviewed *Pagan Religions*, reaching similar conclusions:

> On the one side we have the objective academic, anxious to check facts, to give cautious warnings, and to expound reasonable inferences from known data. But, on the other side, he has interwoven a web of what can only be seen as prejudice against most New Age and pagan thinking. His animus against these and against ideas of Goddess spirituality strike me as extremely non-academic and full of the very suppositions and assumptions that he says he is concerned to oppose.

---

[283] Dashu 1998.

[284] From Hutton's response to Dashu's article, which appeared on the now defunct Crooked Heath website.

Long finds many faults with the book, among them a prejudice against 'alternative' researchers.[285]

A third critique of that book comes from Don Frew in an article examining methodological flaws in studies of historical and modern witchcraft, in particular studies by Aidan Kelly, Jacqueline Simpson and Ronald Hutton.[286] Specific charges levelled against Hutton include misrepresenting Margaret Murray to make her seem more dogmatic and manipulative than she actually was; over-reliance on secondary sources; and making inaccurate generalisations, such as Hutton's statement that religion was always distinct from magic in the ancient world.[287]

Hutton's response to Frew's article is extremely bitter, lambasting it as a "negative process" of fault-finding, an attempt to exonerate Murray and Gardner and discredit himself, Simpson and Kelly: "At no point does he [Frew] grant any of his victims credit for virtues in other writings, or leave them any dignity as scholars; the destructive effect is apparently intended to be total."[288] Hutton's lengthy rebuttal is largely beside the point, though, because from the start he misrepresents Frew's arguments. Frew is quite clear in his agreement that Gardner's and Murray's theories were flawed; his point is that statements they never made and theories they never held have been spuriously attributed to them, and that once these are taken out of the picture it becomes harder to accuse them of wilful deceit.

Frew's observation that theurgy blurred religion and magic is misrepresented by Hutton as a claim that "it was unnecessary to discuss the relationship between religion and magic". Hutton then states in his own defence that "a clear boundary between religion and magic is impossible to find", as though this was not exactly the point Frew was trying to make! Such a graceless admission of error is made even more surreal by the fact that, having been accused of discrediting an author through misrepresentation, Hutton has proceeded to discredit the very author of this accusation, by blatantly misrepresenting him.[289]

---

[285] Long 1992.

[286] Frew 1998. Frew is a Gardnerian High Priest, a long-serving interfaith representative, and one of two US national representatives for the Covenant of the Goddess. He is also a Research Associate of U.C. Berkeley's Central Asia/Silk Road Religion Project. It was in Frew's coven that Aidan Kelly (author of a polemical anti-Gardnerian history of Wicca) first received Gardnerian initiation, and Frew is now one of Kelly's strongest critics.

[287] This last point regarding magic and religion we have already touched on in an earlier chapter.

[288] Hutton 2000. Though he levels some important criticisms, Frew's article is hardly a personal attack, and it is untrue that he never grants his "victims" credit for virtues elsewhere: Lotte Motz, for example, he credits with having written an "otherwise fascinating book". Hutton's characterisation of him as "gladiatorial" is unwarranted, especially given Hutton's own approach in the exchange. When Hutton complains of a "negative process" of fault-finding, one might gently remind him of his own treatment of Charles Leland, Jani Farrell-Roberts (below) and Frew himself.

[289] By the time of writing *Triumph*, Hutton had accepted Frew's point on theurgy (1999a 83) and in *Witches, Druids and King Arthur* he even credits Frew for having alerted him to certain areas of research

Hutton had a similar altercation with Jani Farrell-Roberts over the question of whether Margaret Murray had excised fantastical elements from witch testimonies to make them more believable. Again, rather than engaging with Farrell-Roberts' evidence (which was clear and simple), he instead attacked her character and qualifications, and claimed she was trying unfairly to discredit him: "she is a self-employed investigative journalist, and they are probably the only people in society to whom such behaviour seeks [sic] both natural and praiseworthy".[290] Ironically, during this same altercation Hutton mentions that "one of the discoveries that shocked me about Margaret Murray was the way in which she mobilised academic prejudice against [C. H. L'Estrange Ewen] to get his work ignored".[291] He might consider that perhaps Murray was — like him — simply heavily invested in her cause.

Hutton's theories have also received occasional criticism from scholars outside of Neopaganism. In 2004 he was roundly criticised for publishing a "polemical" article in the *Times Literary Supplement* claiming that the Lindow Man could no longer be considered a victim of human sacrifice. Dr. J. D. Hill, curator of the British and European Iron Age at the British Museum and custodian of the Lindow Man, accused Hutton of selective use of evidence and a failure to take into account new understandings of British and European Iron Age religious practices that have emerged in the last 20 years, which support the original hypothesis of a ritual death. Hill also pointed out the inappropriateness of initiating these claims in a popular magazine rather than a peer-reviewed academic journal.[292]

That *Triumph* has not had more critical attention from academia may largely be explained by the obscurity of the subject, cutting as it does across so many rarely-combined areas of academic research. Indeed, writing on a subject traditionally shunned by academics, Hutton was criticised more for "having sold out to the witches" than for any factual errors. He has mentioned the "loneliness of the work [of writing *Triumph*] and the suspicion or derision of academic colleagues". Few of his peers took his topic of research seriously, and probably fewer still, if any, were competent to critically review the book. According to him he could not find "a single other academic historian with a Pagan background in Britain, and so if the branches of modern paganism were to be recognised as having a 'genuine' history, I would have to take on the job without any support or companionship within my profession."[293]

(2003a 316, 320, 324), but to my knowledge he has never yet retracted his vilification of him.

[290] Hutton 2003b 14.

[291] Hutton 2003b 11.

[292] Hill 2004.

[293] Hutton 2003b 15. In *Triumph* he quotes his student, Owen Davies, as stating in 1995 that it "is generally considered that witchcraft and magic is not a relevant or even a valid field of research for the modern historian" (Hutton 1999a 84) — presumably referring to the *practice* of witchcraft, rather than the persecution of it, since the latter was by then a well-established field of historical research.

Conclusion

Despite the many disagreements I have with Hutton, our views on the origins of Wicca probably have a lot in common. True, I would trace these origins a generation or two further back before Gardner, since the evidence for his initiation into an existing coven now seems quite strong; but these forebears of his seem to have come from ceremonial backgrounds, and their connection with witchcraft was probably more through perceived past life memories than through any surviving tradition.[294] To my mind there is a strong Rosicrucian (or perhaps Neoplatonic?) element in Wicca, an added flavour different to the ecstatic shamanism we glimpse in historical witchcraft. And Gardner and Valiente doubtless added much to the fragmentary rites they received — both admitted their rôles in rewriting the rituals we have today.[295]

None of this is to say that there were not other surviving traditions of witchcraft. Numerous people have claimed that their families preserved such traditions, and I am inclined to believe that some at least are telling the truth. One of the most striking pieces of evidence for late survival is a series of pits discovered at Saveock Water, Cornwall, from 2003 onwards. These pits were carefully lined with bird or animal skins (fur or feathers facing inwards), inside of which were placed pebbles, bird claws, dozens of eggs containing chicks close to hatching (one pit held fifty-five), dead magpies, cat claws and teeth, and other objects, including a seven-inch iron disc covered with swan skin on one side and animal fur on the other.

On the same site were two spring-fed, quartz-lined pools in which had been deposited a large assortment of offerings, ranging from pins and pieces of cloth to hair and nail clippings, heather branches, and even a fragment of a cauldron! Radiocarbon dating shows the various pits were made at different times: the oldest ones, lined with swan skins, date from c. 1640, but a pit lined with cat skin dates from the 1740s to 1780s, and one lined with dog skin (containing the iron disk, among its other con-

---

[294] Heselton 2000; 2003. There is still a possibility that within the New Forest Coven the Mason family were hereditary witches (Heselton 2000 101–114), though how complete a tradition they preserved is impossible to tell.

[295] Valiente 2007 57–62.

tents) dates from post-1950! A family of witches were reputed to live on a neighbouring property until the 1980s. A connection between these pits and the goddess Brigit (or the later St. Brighid) has been postulated, since she is closely associated with swans; aside from the swan pelts and the swan-skin on the disc, small pebbles found in one pit prove to have come from Swan Pool, fifteen miles downriver from the site.[296]

As suggestive as all this may be, my intention in this article is not to champion any particular theory regarding the origins of modern witchcraft. I am limiting myself for the time-being to critiquing Hutton's account and providing counter-examples, but not proposing an alternative history of my own. I hope merely to re-open lines of inquiry that I believe should never have been closed, and to defend those who find themselves marginalised for questioning orthodoxy — which is what Hutton's work has become. There is a growing tendency among the more caustic of his followers to ridicule 'alternative' researchers, applying labels such as 'Murrayite', 'Feminist', 'non-academic' and 'polemicist' as convenient black marks — a license to dismiss a person's work without evaluating their evidence. Such *ad hominem* attacks are a poor substitute for reasoned debate, and rather than progressing our understanding of history they merely entrench the received 'wisdom' and turn history into a religion.

The upshot is that a single balanced and reliable source for the history of modern witchcraft does not yet exist. Hutton's books contain much to enlighten, but just as much to mislead, and they cannot be treated as a straightforward, objective summary of the topic. Until a better work appears, the student will face a stack of books[297] and a multitude of details, sometimes conflicting, and never to be discounted prematurely. It will take hard work and a critical eye. I hope this small book of mine will help others navigate this task, and I urge them to evaluate my own claims just as carefully as they do Hutton's or anyone else's. History is a tattered, delicate and very precious fabric, and we should approach it with the patience and care of an archivist, gently teasing out whatever threads of knowledge we can. We cannot take shears to it, no matter how much tidier it might look after a trim or how well the shape we have cut out might suit us.

---

[296] Ravilious 2008; Wood 2005.

[297] The most important to read are probably Philip Heselton's *Wiccan Roots* (2000) and *Gerald Gardner and the Cauldron of Inspiration* (2003), and Carlo Ginzburg's *Ecstasies* (1990). Nigel Pennick and Prudence Jones' *A History of Pagan Europe* (1995) provides a very useful and mostly reliable summary of pre- and post-Christian paganism, and P. G. Maxwell-Stuart's *Witchcraft in Europe and the New World, 1400–1800* (2001) is a very concise introduction to the witch-trials, which could be supplemented by a larger volume such as *Early Modern Witchcraft: Centres and Peripheries* edited by Bengt Ankarloo and Gustav Henningsen (1989). Michael Howard's *Modern Wicca: A History from Gerald Gardner to the Present* (2010) is a valuable source for more recent events, but may not always be entirely accurate, if his account of my mother-coven in New Zealand is anything to go by.

One point Hutton and I certainly agree on is that Wicca and its various off-shoots have value regardless of their origins. As a priest of the Goddess and God no historian can take away what I've learnt and experienced, or the joy and wisdom I've found within the Craft. I'm well aware that the founders of our religion were flawed people (as am I), and yet they have bequeathed to us a thing of great value. And here is one of the mysteries that priesthood reveals to us: through our training we become more sensitive to the faults and oddities of the human personality — our own and others' — and yet we also begin to see how this imperfect human vehicle can paradoxically express divinity, and be a channel for great inspiration, energy and beauty. Sincere or cynical, having once offered our service to the Gods there is every chance that we will deliver, and wittingly or unwittingly be drawn to their work. The founders of our cult were imperfect, and Hutton is imperfect too; and if ever Hutton was inspired to honour the Goddess in some way, I think She has taken him up on the offer: he says his book is a triumph for the Moon, and perhaps it shall prove so, for it stands as a challenge to all the Craft, an incitement to us to seek the real truth.

★

Bibliography

Aldhouse-Green, Miranda Jane (1992) *Symbol and Image in Celtic Religious Art*. London: Routledge.

Alver, Bente (2008) *Mellem mennesker og magter: Magi i hekseforfølgelsernes tid*. Oslo: Scandinavian Academic Press.

Ankarloo, Bengt (1989) "Sweden: The Mass Burnings (1668–1676)" in Ankarloo & Henningsen (eds.) *Early Modern European Witchcraft: Centres and Peripheries*. Oxford: Clarendon Press.

Ankarloo, Bengt & Henningsen, Gustav (1989) *Early Modern European Witchcraft: Centres and Peripheries*. Oxford: Clarendon Press.

Ashmand, J. M. (1822) *Ptolemy's Tetrabiblos, or Quadripartite: Being Four Books of the Influence of the Stars*. London: Davis & Dickson.

Athenaeus; transl. Yonge, C. D. (1854) *The Deipnosophists, or Banquet of the Learned*. London: Henry G. Bohn.

Athanassakis, Apostolos (1988) *The Orphic Hymns: Text, Translation and Notes*. Atlanta: Society of Biblical Literature.

Babayan, Kathryn (2002) *Mystics, Monarchs and Messiahs*. Cambridge, MA: Harvard University Center for Middle-Eastern Studies.

Balas, Edith (1995) *Michelangelo's Medici Chapel: A New Interpretation*. Darby, PA: DIANE Publishing.

Barandiarán, José Miguel de; ed. Altuna, Jesús; transl. Fornhoff, F. H. & White, L. (2009) *Selected writings of José Miguel de Barandiarán: Basque prehistory and ethnography*. Reno, NV: University of Nevada Press.

Baroja, Julio Caro (1968) *The World of Witches*. Chicago: University of Chicago Press.

Bayley, Harold (2003) *Lost Language of Symbolism* Vol. 1. Whitefish, MT: Kessinger Publishing.

Behringer, Wolfgang (1998) *Shaman of Oberstdorf: Chonrad Stoeckhlin and the Phantoms of the Night*. Charlottesville, VA: University Press of Virginia.

Berger, Pamela (2001) *The Goddess Obscured: Transformation of the Grain Protectress from Goddess to Saint*. Boston: Beacon Press.

Betegh, Gábor (2004) *The Derveni Papyrus: Cosmology, Theology and Interpretation*. Cambridge: Cambridge University Press.

Betz, Hans Dieter (1992) *The Greek Magical Papyri in Translation, Including the Demotic Spells: Book I: Texts*. Chicago: University of Chicago Press.

Beza, Marcu (1928) *Paganism in Romanian Folklore*. New York, NY: E. P. Dutton & Co.

Bonnefoy, Yves & Doniger, Wendy (1992a) *Greek and Egyptian Mythologies*. Chicago: University of Chicago Press.

Bonnefoy, Yves & Doniger, Wendy (1992b) *Roman and European Mythologies*. Chicago: University of Chicago Press.

Borgeaud, Philippe; transl. Atlass, K. & Redfield, J. (1988) *The Cult of Pan In Ancient Greece*. Chicago: University of Chicago Press.

Briggs, Robin (1995) *Communities of Belief: Cultural and Social Tension in Early Modern France*. Oxford: Oxford University Press.

Budge, E. A. Wallis (1904) *The Gods of the Egyptians, or, Studies in Egyptian Mythology*. London: Methuen & Co. Ltd.

Budge, E. A. Wallis (2003) *Osiris or The Egyptian Religion of Resurrection*. Whitefish, MT: Kessinger Publishing.

Budge, E. A. Wallis (1934) *From Fetish to God in Ancient Egypt*. Oxford: Oxford University Press.

Bunson, Matthew (1995) *A Dictionary of the Roman Empire*. New York, NY: Oxford University Press US.

Burkert, Walter (1985) *Greek Religion*. Cambridge, MA: Harvard University Press.

Chambers, Edmund Kerchever (1996) *The Medieval Stage*. New York, NY: Courier Dover Publications.

Chuvin, Pierre (1990) *A Chronicle of the Last Pagans*. Cambridge, MA: Harvard University Press.

Cohn, Norman (1975) *Europe's Inner Demons*. London: Chatto-Heinemann.

Crawford, J. R. (1967) *Witchcraft and Sorcery in Rhodesia*. Oxford: Oxford University Press.

Crook, J.A., Lintott, Andrew & Rawson, Elizabeth (1923) *The Cambridge Ancient History*. Vol. 9. Cambridge: Cambridge University Press.

Darmesteter, James (tr.) (1882) *The Zend Avesta, Part II: The Sîrôzahs, Yasts and Nyâyis*. Oxford: Oxford University Press.

Dashu, Max (1998) *A Review of Ronald Hutton's The Pagan Religions of the Ancient British Isles*. http://www.suppressedhistories.net/articles/hutton_review.html

Dashu, Max (1999) "Another View of the Witch Hunts" in *The Pomegranate* Issue 9.

Davidson, H. R. Ellis (1965) *Gods and Myths of Northern Europe*. London: Penguin Books.

Dawkins, R. M. (1906) "The Modern Carnival in Thrace and the Cult of Dionysus" in *The Journal of Hellenic Studies* Vol. 26 pp. 191–206.

DeBolt, Darien C. (1998) *George Gemistos Plethon on God: Heterodoxy in Defense of Orthodoxy*. Paper delivered at the Twentieth World Congress of Philosophy, Boston, MA, August 1998.

Delia, Diana (1998) "Isis, or the Moon". In *Orientalia Lovaniensia Analecta: Egyptian Religion: The Last Thousand Years*. Part 1. Leuven: Peeters Publishers.

Dickie, Matthew W. (2003) *Magic and Magicians in the Greco-Roman World*. London: Routledge.

Dierkens, Alain (1998) "The Evidence of Archaeology" in Milis, Ludo J. R. (ed.) *The Pagan Middle Ages*. Woodbridge, Suffolk: Boydell.

Diodorus Siculus; transl. Oldfather, C. H. (1933) *The Library of History* Vol. 1. Loeb Classical Library. Cambridge, MA: Harvard University Press.

Dorcey, Peter F. (1992) *The Cult of Silvanus: A Study in Roman Folk Religion*. Leiden: Brill.

Dronke, Ursula (1992) "Völuspá and the Sibylline Traditions" in North, R. & Hofstra, T. (eds.) *Latin Culture and Medieval Germanic Europe: Proceedings from the First Germania Latina Conference Held at the University of Groningen, 26 May 1989 (Mediaevalia Groningana)*. Amsterdam: John Benjamins Pub. Co.

Duerr, Hans Peter (1985) *Dreamtime: Concerning the Boundary between Wilderness and Civilization*. New York, NY: Basil Blackwell.

Evans, Arthur J. (1901) "Crete: The Neolithic Settlement at Knossos and Its Place in the History of Early Aegean Culture" in *Man* vol. 1 pp. 183–5. London: The Anthropological Institute.

Evans, Arthur J. (1921) *The Palace of Minos: A Comparative Account of the Successive Stages of the Early Cretan Civilization as Illustrated by the Discoveries at Knossos*. Vol. I. London: MacMillan & Co, Ltd.

Evans-Pritchard, Edward Evan (1937) *Witchcraft, Oracles and Magic Among the Azande*. Oxford: Oxford University Press.

Ewen, C. L'Estrange (1929) *Witch Hunting and Witch Trials*. London: K. Paul.

Ewen, C. L'Estrange (1933) *Witchcraft and Demonianism*. London: Heath, Cranton, Ltd.

Farrell-Roberts, Jani (2003a) "A New or Old Western Paganism?" In *The Cauldron* 108.

Farrell-Roberts, Jani (2003b) "A New or Old Western Paganism? The Controversy Over Margaret Murray, Part Two" In *The Cauldron* 109.

Faulkner, R., Goelet, O., Andrews, C., Von Dassow, E. & Wasserman, J. (2008) *The Egyptian Book of the Dead*. San Francisco: Chronicle Books.

Fees, Craig (1989) "Mummers and Momoeri: A Response" in *Folklore* vol. 100:ii pp. 240–247.

Ficino, Marsilio; transl. Allen, Michael J. B. (2008) *Commentaries on Plato: Phaedrus & Ion*. Cambridge, MA: Harvard University Press.

Fisher, W. B., Gershevitch, I., Yarshater, E., Frye, R. N., Boyle, J. A., Jackson, P., Lockhart, L., Avery, P., Hambly, G., Melville, C. (1968) *The Cambridge History of Iran*. Cambridge: Cambridge University Press.

Fitzgerald, David (1885) "Early Celtic History and Mythology" in *Revue Celtique* vol. 6. Paris: F. Vieweg.

Frew, Donald H. (1998) "Methodological Flaws in Recent Studies of Historical and Modern Witchcraft". *Ethnologies* Issue 1. Canadian Folklore Association.

Frew, Donald H. (1999) "Harran: Last Refuge of Classical Paganism" in *The Pomegranate* Issue 9.

Gallop, Rodney (1936) *Portugal: A Book of Folk-ways*. New York, NY: The Macmillan Co.

Gardner, Gerald (2004) *Witchcraft Today*. New York, NY: Citadel Press

Ghinoiu, Ion (date unknown) *Dragaica – Sanzienele* [Romanian].
http://www.crestinortodox.ro/datini-obiceiuri-si-superstitii/68804-dragaica-sanzienele

Gibbons, Jenny (1998) "Recent Developments in the Study of the Great European Witch Hunt" in *The Pomegranate* Issue 5.

Gibbons, Jenny (2000) Letter to the editor in *The Pomegranate* Issue 12.

Ginzburg, Carlo; transl. Tedeschi, John (1983) *The Night Battles: Witchcraft & Agrarian Cults in the Sixteenth and Seventeenth Centuries*. Baltimore, MD: Johns Hopkins University Press.

Ginzburg, Carlo; transl. Rosenthal, R. (1990) *Ecstasies: Deciphering the Witches' Sabbath*. London: Hutchinson Radius.

Godwin, Joscelyn (1979) *Athanasius Kircher*. London: Thames and Hudson.

Godwin, Joscelyn (2005) *The Pagan Dream of the Renaissance*. Boston, MA: Weiser Books.

Gollnick, James (1999) *The Religious Dreamworld of Apuleius' Metamorphoses: Recovering a Forgotten Hermeneutic*. Waterloo, ON: Wilfrid Laurier University Press.

Gottheil, Richard (1906) "Eliseus". In *The Jewish Encyclopedia*. New York, NY: Funk and Wagnalls.

Graves, Robert (1961) *The White Goddess: A Historical Grammar of Poetic Myth*. London: Faber & Faber.

Green, Tamara M. (1992) *The City of the Moon God*. Leiden: E. J. Brill.

Griffiths, Gordon (1988) "Classical Greece and the Italian Renaissance" in Thomas, Carol G. (ed.) *Paths from Ancient Greece*. Leiden: E. J. Brill.

Griffiths, John Gwyn (1975) *The Isis Book, Metamorphoses XI*. Leiden: Brill Archive.

Grimm, Jacob; transl. Stallybrass, S. (1998) *Teutonic Mythology*. New York, NY: Courier Dover Publications.

Hard, Robin & Rose, Herbert Jennings (2004) *The Routledge Handbook of Greek Mythology*. London: Routledge.

Harrison, Jane Ellen (1903) "Mystica Vannus Iacchi" in *The Journal of Hellenic Studies* Vol. 23 pp. 292–324.

Harrison, Jane Ellen (1928) *Myths of Greece and Rome*. Garden City, NY: Doubleday, Doran & Co.

Harrison, Jane Ellen (1991). *Prolegomena to the Study of Greek Religion*. Princeton, NJ: Princeton University Press.

Henningsen, Gustav (1989) "'The Ladies From Outside': An Archaic Pattern of the Witches' Sabbath" in Ankarloo & Henningsen (eds.) *Early Modern European Witchcraft: Centres and Peripheries*. Oxford: Clarendon Press.

Heselton (2000) *Wiccan Roots*. Chieveley, Berkshire: Capall Bann Publishing.

Heselton (2003) *Gerald Gardner and the Cauldron of Inspiration*. Chieveley, Berkshire: Capall Bann Publishing.

Hill, J. D. (2004) "A Reply to Ronald Hutton's Commentary 'What did Happen to Lindow Man?'" TLS Jan 30th" in *The Times Literary Supplement*, 7 Feb 2004.

Howard, Michael (2010) *Modern Wicca: A History from Gerald Gardner to the Present*. Woodbury, MN: Llewellyn.

Hutton, Ronald (1991) *Pagan Religions of the Ancient British Isles*. Oxford: Blackwell Publishing.

Hutton, Ronald (1996) *Stations of the Sun: A history of the ritual year in Britain*. Oxford: Oxford University Press.

Hutton, Ronald (1999a) *The Triumph of the Moon: A History of Modern Pagan Witchcraft*. Oxford: Oxford University Press.

Hutton, Ronald (1999b) "Modern Pagan Witchcraft" in de Blécourt, W., Hutton, R., La Fontaine, J. S. & Ankarloo, B. *Witchcraft and Magic in Europe*. London: Continuum International.

Hutton, Ronald (2000) "Paganism and Polemic: The Debate Over the Origins of Modern Pagan Witchcraft" in *Folklore*, April 2000.

Hutton, Ronald (2001) *Shamans: Siberian Spirituality and the Western Imagination*. London: Hambledon and London.

Hutton, Ronald (2003a) *Witches, Druids and King Arthur*. London: Hambledon & London.

Hutton, Ronald (2003b) "The Great Debate" in *The Cauldron* May 2003.

Hutton, Ronald (2009a) "Afterword" in Evans, D. & Green, D. (eds.) *Ten Years of Triumph of the Moon*. LaVergne, TN: Hidden Publishing.

Hutton, Ronald (2009b) "Dion Fortune and Wicca". Address delivered at *Dion Fortune Seminar 2009*, Glastonbury Town Hall. http://companyofavalon.net/documents/RonaldHuttonaddress.DF.doc

Idel, Moshe (2002) "Prisca Theologia in Marsilio Ficino" in Allen, M., Rees, V. & Davies, M. (eds.) *Marsilio Ficino: His Theology, His Philosophy, His Legacy*. Leiden: Brill.

Idel, Moshe (2008) "Johannes Reuchlin: Kabbalah, Pythagorean Philosophy and Modern Scholarship" in *Studia Judaica* XVI, Dr. Moshe Carmilly Institute for Hebrew and Jewish History. Cluj-Napoca: Babeş-Bolyai University.

Jeep, John M. (2001) *Medieval Germany: An Encyclopedia*. London: Routledge.

Jones, Prudence & Pennick, Nigel (1997) *A History of Pagan Europe*. London: Routledge.

Kahk, Juhan (1989) "Estonia II: The Crusade Against Idolatry" in Ankarloo & Henningsen (eds.) *Early Modern European Witchcraft: Centres and Peripheries*. Oxford: Clarendon Press.

Kaspersen, Søren & Haastrup, Ulla (2004) *Images of Cult and Devotion: Function and Reception of Christian Images in Medieval and Post-Medieval Europe*. Copenhagen: Museum Tusculanum Press.

Kennedy, Peter (1980) *Folktracks FSD-60-107 Step In, Wild Horse* [CD]. Portishead, Bristol: Folktracks Publications.

King, Francis X. (1975) *Magic: The Western Tradition*. London: Thames and Hudson.

Klaniczay, Gábor & Pócs, Éva (2005) *Communicating with the Spirits*, Vol. 1. Budapest: Central European University Press.

Kligman, Gail (1977) *Căluş: Symbolic Transformation in Romanian Ritual*. Chicago: University of Chicago Press.

Koch, John T. (2006) Celtic Culture: A Historical Encyclopedia. Santa Barbara, CA: ABC-CLIO.

Kure, Henning (2006) "Hanging on the World Tree: Man and Cosmos in Old Norse Mythic Poetry" in Andrén, A., Jennbert, K. & Raudvere, C. (eds.) *Old Norse Religion in Long Term Perspectives: Origins, Changes and Interactions, an International Conference in Lund, Sweden, June 3–7, 2004*. Lund: Nordic Academic Press.

Kvideland, R. & Sehmsdorf, H. K. (eds.) (1988) *Scandinavian Folk Belief and Legend*. Minneapolis, MN: University of Minnesota Press.

Lamond, Fred (2004) *Fifty Years of Wicca*. Sutton Mallet, Somerset: Green Magic.

Lawson, John Cuthbert (2003) *Modern Greek Folklore and Ancient Greek Religion: A Study In Survivals*. Whitefish, MT: Kessinger Publishing.

Lederer, David (2002) "Living With the Dead: Ghosts in Early Modern Bavaria" in Edwards, Kathryn A. (ed.) *Werewolves, Witches and Wandering Spirits: Traditional Belief and Folklore in Early Modern Europe*. Kirksville, MO: Truman State University Press.

Leeming, David Adams (1998) *Mythology: The Voyage of the Hero*. Oxford: Oxford University Press.

Leland, Charles G. (1892) *Etruscan Roman Remains In Popular Tradition*. London: T. Fisher Unwin.

Leland, Charles G. (1899) *Aradia, or the Gospel of the Witches*. London: David Nutt.

Leland, Charles G.; ed. Pazzaglini, Mario & Pazzaglini, Dina (1998) *Aradia, or the Gospel of the Witches*. With additional material by Chas S. Clifton, Robert Mathiesen and Robert E Chartowich, foreword by by Stewart Farrar. Blaine, WA: Phoenix Publishing Inc.

Lindow, John (2002) *Norse Mythology: A Guide to the Gods, Heroes, Rituals and Beliefs*. Oxford: Oxford University Press.

Long, Asphodel P. (1992) Review in *Wood and Water* 39, Summer.

Luck, Georg (1985) *Arcana Mundi: Magic and the Occult in the Greek and Roman Worlds: A Collection of Ancient Texts*. Baltimore, MD: Johns Hopkins University Press.

Macfarlane, Alan (1970) *Witchcraft in Tudor and Stuart England: A Regional and Comparative Study*. London: Routledge & Kegan Paul.

Mackey, Albert Gallatin (1912) *An Encyclopedia of Freemasonry and Its Kindred Sciences*. Chicago: The Masonic History Company.

MacMullen, Ramsey (1997) *Christianity and Paganism in the Fourth to Eighth Centuries*. New Haven, CT: Yale University Press.

Macrobius; transl. Davies, P. V. (1969) *Saturnalia*. New York, NY: Columbia University Press.

Magliocco, Sabina (2004) *Witching Culture: Folklore and Neo-Paganism in America*. Philadelphia, PA: University of Pennsylvania Press.

Magliocco, Sabina (2009) "Aradia in Sardinia: The Archaeology of a Folk Character" in Evans, D. & Green, D. (eds.) *Ten Years of Triumph of the Moon*. LaVergne, TN: Hidden Publishing.

Mallory, James P. & Adams, Douglas Q. (1997) *Encyclopedia of Indo-European Culture*. London: Routledge.

Marcovich, Miroslav (1988) *Studies in Graeco-Roman Religions and Gnosticism* Vol. 4. Leiden: Brill.

Marculescu, Cristina (year unknown) *Noaptea de Sanziene* [Romanian].
http://www.crestinortodox.ro/datini-obiceiuri-si-superstitii/68734-noaptea-de-sanziene

Mardock, James D. (2008) *Our Scene is London: Ben Jonson's City and the Space of the Author*. London: Routledge.

Massey, Gerald (2007) *Natural Genesis* Vol. I. New York, NY: Cosimo Inc.

Mathiesen, Robert (1998) "Charles G. Leland and the Witches of Italy: The Origin of Aradia" in Leland, C., Pazzaglini, M., Pazzaglini, D., Clifton, C., Mathiesen, R. & Chartowich, R. *Aradia, or the Gospel of the Witches: A New Translation*. Blaine, WA: Phoenix Publishing.

Maxwell-Stuart, P. G. (2001) *Witchcraft in Europe and the New World, 1400-1800*. Basingstoke, Hampshire: Palgrave Macmillan Ltd.

McLean, Adam (1994) *The Magical Calendar: A Synthesis of Magical Symbolism from the Seventeenth-Century Renaissance of Medieval Occultism*. Grand Rapids, MI: Phanes Press.

Mettinger, Tryggve N. D. (2001) *The Riddle of Resurrection: "Dying and Rising Gods" in the Ancient near East*. Philadelphia, PA: Coronet Books.

Midelfort, H. C. Erik (1972) *Witch-hunting in South-Western Germany 1562-1684: The Social and Intellectual Foundations*. Palo Alto, CA: Stanford University Press.

Milis, Ludo J. R. (ed.) (1998) *The Pagan Middle Ages*. Woodbridge, Suffolk: Boydell.

Millington, Peter (2002) *The Origins and Development of English Folk Plays* [Ph.D. thesis]. National Centre for English Cultural Tradition, University of Sheffield.

Mojsov, Bojana (2005) *Osiris: Death and Afterlife of a God*. Hoboken, NJ: Wiley-Blackwell.

Monter, E. William (1976) *Witchcraft in France and Switzerland*. London: Cornell University Press.

Monter, E. William (1982) Review of "Hexenprozesse in Deutschland" by Gerhard Schormann. In *American Historical Review* 87:1407, December 1982.

Morford, Mark P. O. & Lenardon, Robert J. (2006) *Classical Mythology* 7th Edn.. Oxford: Oxford University Press.

Morgan, Gareth (1989) "Mummers and Momoeri" in *Folklore* vol. 100:i pp. 84–87.

Motz, Lotte (1984) "The Winter Goddess: Percht, Holda, and Related Figures" in *Folklore* vol. 95:ii, 1984.

Muchembled, Robert (1989) "Satanic Myths and Cultural Reality" in Ankarloo & Henningsen (eds.) *Early Modern European Witchcraft: Centres and Peripheries*. Oxford: Clarendon Press.

Murray, Margaret (1963) *The Witch-Cult in Western Europe*. Oxford: Oxford University Press.

Nonnos; transl. Rouse, W. H. D. (1940) *Dionysiaca* (3 volumes). Loeb Classical Library. Cambridge, MA: Harvard University Press.

Ogier, Darryl (1998) "Night revels and werewolfery in Calvinist Guernsey", in *Folklore,* 1998 Annual.

Otto, Walter Friedrich (1995) *Dionysus: Myth and Cult*. Bloomington, IN: Indiana University Press.

Page, Raymond Ian (2006) *An Introduction to English Runes*. Woodbridge, Suffolk: Boydell Press.

Pausanias; transl. Jones, W. H. S. & Omerod, H. A. (1918) *Description of Greece*. Cambridge, MA: Harvard University Press.

Parker, Robert (1995) "Early Orphism" in Powell, Anton (ed.) *The Greek World*. London: Routledge.

Parker, Robert (2005) *Polytheism and society at Athens*. Oxford: Oxford University Press.

Patrick, James (2007) *Renaissance and Reformation*. Tarrytown, NY: Marshall Cavendish.

Patton, Kimberley Christine (2009) *Religion of the Gods: Ritual, Paradox and Reflexivity*. Oxford: Oxford University Press.

Pazzaglini, M. (1998a) "Leland and the Magical World of Aradia" in Leland, C., Pazzaglini, M., Pazzaglini, D., Clifton, C., Mathiesen, R. & Chartowich, R. *Aradia, or the Gospel of the Witches: A New Translation*. Blaine, WA: Phoenix Publishing.

Pazzaglini, M. (1998b) "Research Notes" in Leland, C., Pazzaglini, M., Pazzaglini, D., Clifton, C., Mathiesen, R. & Chartowich, R. *Aradia, or the Gospel of the Witches: A New Translation*. Blaine, WA: Phoenix Publishing.

Pegge, Samuel (1874) "An Alphabet of Kenticisms" in *Archaeologia Cantiana* vol. 9. London: Mitchell & Hughes for the Kent Archaeological Society.

Pennick, Nigel & Jones, Prudence (1995) *A History of Pagan Europe*. London: Routledge.

Petreska, Vesna (2005) "Demons of Fate in Macedonian Folk Beliefs" in Gábor Klaniczay & Éva Pócs (eds.) *Christian Demonology and Popular Mythology*. Budapest: Central European University Press.

Pina-Cabral, João de (1992) "The Gods of the Gentiles are Demons: The Problem of Pagan Survivals in European Culture" in Hastrup, Kirsten (ed.) *Other Histories*. London: Routledge.

Pitts, John Linwood (1886) *Witchcraft and Devil Lore in the Channel Islands*. Guernsey: Guille-Alles Library.

Pliny the Elder; transl. Bostock, J. & Riley, H.T. (1855) *The Natural History*. London: Taylor & Francis.

Plutarch; transl. King, Charles William (1882) "On Isis and Osiris" in *Plutarch's Morals: Theosophical Essays*. London: George Bell.

Pócs, Éva (1999) *Between the Living and the Dead*. Budapest: Central European University Press.

Poole, Robert (ed.) (2003) *The Lancashire Witches: Histories and Stories*. Manchester: Manchester University Press.

Powell, F. (1903) "In Memoriam. Charles Godfrey Leland", in *Folk-Lore* vol. 14, pp. 162–164.

Purkiss, Diane (1996) *The Witch In History: Early Modern and Twentieth-century Representations*. London: Routledge.

Rappoport, Philippa (1999) "If It Dries Out, It's No Good: Women, Hair and Rusalki Beliefs". In *Slavic and East European Folklore Association Journal* Vol. 4 no. 1. pp. 55–64.

Ravilious, Kate (2008) "Witches of Cornwall" in *Archaeology* vol. 61 no. 6. Archaeological Institute of America.

Rees, Roger (2002) *Layers of Loyalty in Latin Panegyric, AD 289-307*. Oxford: Oxford University Press.

Regardie, Israel (1989) *The Golden Dawn* 6th edition. Woodbury, MN: Llewellyn Publishing.

Riches, Samantha (2000) *St. George: Hero, Martyr and Myth*. Stroud, Gloucestershire: Sutton Publishing.

Robinson, Kate (2005) "The Celestial Streams of Giulio Camillo". In *History of Science* Vol. 43, pp. 321–341.

Rohde, Eleanour Sinclair (1922) *The Old English Herbals*. London: Longmans, Green & Co.

Roller, Lynn E. (1999) *In Search of God the Mother*. Berkeley: University of California Press.

Rose, Elliot (2003) *A Razor for a Goat: Problems in the History of Witchcraft and Diabolism*. Toronto: University of Toronto Press.

Ross, Anne (1967) *Pagan Celtic Britain: Studies in Iconography and Tradition*. London: Routledge & Kegan Paul.

Russell, Jeffrey Burton (1972) *Witchcraft in the Middle Ages*. Ithaca, NY: Cornell University Press.

Sanders, Maxine (2008) *Firechild: The Life and Magic of Maxine Sanders 'Witch Queen'*. Oxford: Mandrake of Oxford.

Sarton, George (1993) *Ancient Science Through the Golden Age of Greece*. New York: Courier Dover Publications.

Schormann, Gerhard (1996) *Hexenprozesse in Deutschland*. Göttingen: Vandenhoeck & Ruprecht.

Schouten, Jan (1968) *The Pentagram as a Medical Symbol*. Nieuwkoop: De Graaf.

Scot, Reginald (1989) *The Discoverie of Witchcraft*. New York, NY: Dover Publications.

Sharpe, Samuel (1837) *Rudiments of a Vocabulary of Egyptian Hieroglyphics*. London: Edward Moxon.

Siefker, Phyllis (1996) *Santa Claus: Last of the Wild Men*. Jefferson, NC: McFarland.

Simek, Rudolf (1996) *Dictionary of Northern Mythology*. Cambridge, UK: D. S. Brewer.

Snell, Lionel (1979) *SSOTBME: An Essay on Magic*. New York, NY: Samuel Weiser, Inc.

Solmsen, Friedrich (1979) *Isis Among the Greeks and Romans*. Cambridge, MA: Harvard University Press.

Steiner, Rudolf; transl. Hindes, James (1998) "The Significance of Christmas from the Perspective of Spiritual Science" In *The Christian Mystery*. Blauvelt, NY: Steiner Books.

Stevenson, Ian (2003) *European Cases of the Reincarnation Type*. Jefferson, NC: McFarland.

Strabo; transl. Jones, Horace L. & Sterrett, John R. S. (1989) *Geography*. Loeb Classical Library. Cambridge, MA: Harvard University Press.

Strickland, Agnes & Strickland, Elizabeth (1864) *Lives of the Queens of England, from the Norman Conquest*. Boston, MA: Taggard & Thompson.

Tacitus, Cornelius; transl. Gordon, Thomas (2004) *Tacitus on Germany*. Whitefish, MT: Kessinger Publishing.

Thomas, Keith (1997) *Religion and the Decline of Magic*. Oxford: Oxford University Press.

Turner, Patricia & Coulter, Charles Russell (2001) *Dictionary of Ancient Deities*. Oxford: Oxford University Press.

Twycross, Meg & Carpenter, Sarah (2002) *Masks and Masking in Medieval and Early Tudor England*. Aldershot, Hants.: Ashgate.

Tydeman, William (1979) *The Theatre in the Middle Ages: Western European Stage Conditions, c. 800–1576*. Cambridge: Cambridge University Press.

Valiente, Doreen (1984) "The Search For Old Dorothy" in Farrar, Janet & Stewart, *The Witches' Way*. London: Robert Hale.

Valiente, Doreen (2007) *The Rebirth of Witchcraft*. London: Robert Hale.

Varner, Gary R. (2006) *The Mythic Forest, the Green Man and the Spirit of Nature*. New York, NY: Algora Publishing.

Varner, Gary R. (2008) *Gargoyles, Grotesques and Green Men: Ancient Symbolism in European and American Architecture*. Lulu.com.

Verbrugghe, Gerald & Wickersham, John Moore (2001) *Berossos and Manetho, Introduced and Translated*. Ann Arbor, MI: University of Michigan Press.

Vogel, Cornelia Johanna (1966) *Pythagoras and Early Pythagoreanism: An Interpretation of Neglected Evidence on the Philosopher Pythagoras*. Assen, The Netherlands: Van Gorcum.

Voss, Angela (2002) "Orpheus Redivivus: The Musical Magic of Marsilio Ficino" in Allen, M., Rees, V. & Davies, M. (eds.) *Marsilio Ficino: His Theology, His Philosophy, His Legacy*. Leiden: Brill.

Webb, Ruth (1989) "The *Nomoi* of Gemistos Plethon in the Light of Plato's *Laws*" in *Journal of the Warburg and Courtauld Institutes* vol. 52, pp. 214–9. London: University of London, Warburg Institute.

West, M. L. (1983) *The Orphic Poems*. Oxford: Oxford University Press.

West, M. L. (2007) *Indo-European Poetry and Myth*. Oxford: Oxford University Press.

Wilby, Emma (2005) *Cunning Folk and Familiar Spirits: Shamanistic Visionary Traditions in Early Modern British Witchcraft and Magic*. Brighton: Sussex Academic Press.

Williams, Ifor (1944) *Lectures on Early Welsh Poetry*. Dublin: Dublin Institute for Advanced Studies.

Williams, Stephen (1997) *Diocletian and the Roman Recovery*. London: Routledge.

Witt, Reginald Eldred (1997) *Isis in the Ancient World*. Baltimore, MD: Johns Hopkins University Press.

Wood, Jacqui (2005) *Secret Bird Worshiping Cult at Saveock*. From the Saveock Water Archaeology website: http://www.archaeologyonline.org/Site%20-%20Area%20Feather%20Pits.html

Woodhouse, C. M. (2000) *Gemistos Plethon: The Last of the Hellenes*. Oxford: Clarendon Press.

Wright, Thomas (1862) *The Worship of the Generative Powers: During the Middle Ages of Western Europe*. London: J. C. Hotten.

Yates, Frances A. (1964) *Giordano Bruno and the Hermetic Tradition*. London: Routledge & Kegan Paul.

Zancer, Paul (1990) *The Power of Images in the Age of Augustus*. Ann Arbor, MI: University of Michigan Press.

Index

CPSIA information can be obtained
at www.ICGtesting.com
Printed in the USA
BVHW031350200121
598221BV00001B/130

9 780473 174583